Tarot in
5 Minutes

Your Shortcut to Love, Money, and Happiness

Karina Collins

BENNION
KEARNY

Published in 2019 by Bennion Kearny Limited.
Copyright © Bennion Kearny 2019

ISBN: 978-1-909125-41-4

Karina Collins has asserted her right under the Copyright, Designs and Patents Act, 1988 to be identified as the author of this book.

All Rights Reserved. No part of this publication may be reproduced, stored in a retrieval system, or transmitted in any form or by any means, electronic, mechanical, photocopying, recording or otherwise, without the prior permission of the publisher. This book is sold subject to the condition that it shall not, by way of trade or otherwise, be lent, re-sold, hired out or otherwise circulated without the publisher's prior consent in any form of binding or cover other than that it which it is published and without a similar condition including this condition being imposed on the subsequent purchaser. Bennion Kearny has endeavoured to provide trademark information about all the companies and products mentioned in this book by the appropriate use of capitals. However, Bennion Kearny cannot guarantee the accuracy of this information.

Published by Bennion Kearny Limited, 6 Woodside, Churnet View Road, Oakamoor, ST10 3AE

www.BennionKearny.com

Illustrations from the Aquatic Tarot reproduced by permission of Andreas Schröter. © Andreas Schröter 1995-2004. All rights reserved by Andreas Schröter. Further reproduction prohibited.

With love to Anne and Neil.

Table of Contents

I am really pleased to be able to include reproductions of Andreas
Schröter's beautiful watercolours of the Rider-Waite Tarot deck.

Andreas' wonderful deck is not available commercially, so I recommend
you use the standard Rider-Waite deck with this book
for your own readings.

Karina

Introduction

Tarot is a wonderful tool that anyone can use. It is the maker of dreams and a guiding star.

It is brilliant for anyone looking for a shortcut to success in life. Whoever you are – student, mum, unemployed, entrepreneur, hairdresser or retiree – this book will teach you to read Tarot in less time than it takes to boil an egg.

Questions this book can answer!

- Will I find love?
- Is my relationship over?
- Will I get a new job?
- Will I move house?
- How can I make more money?
- How can I become happier?

Tarot in 5 Minutes is the perfect book for beginners as well as experienced Tarot readers who want clearer answers to their questions.

The book will cover:

- Karina's super-fast 5 Minute Tutorial
- 78 card meanings, radically condensed to give clearer guidance
- 23 sample reading lessons
- Simple to understand, jargon-free writing

Now, let's get started!

> **Karina Says:** There isn't a single person in the world, who does not need this book. I get a headache knowing there are so many people struggling with life when the answers they need are just five minutes away.

The 5 Minute Tutorial

Section 1. The Essentials | Time: 1 Minute

In this section, you will learn about the Tarot and why it works. The better your understanding, the more confident you will be with your readings.

Which Tarot Deck Should I Use?

Many wonderful Tarot decks have been created over the years, and this book uses the beautiful Rider-Waite watercolour paintings of Andreas Schröter to explain the meanings of each card. Andreas' deck is not available commercially, so I recommend you use the traditional Rider-Waite deck for your own readings. This particular deck is steeped in history and has the collective goodwill of generations of users behind it.

How Does The Tarot Work?

How is it possible that a deck of cards knows the answers to your questions? Is there an all-knowing *intelligence* directing the cards as you shuffle? Perhaps, but the truth is, no-one knows for sure. The only thing we know for certain is that the Tarot has been popular for hundreds of years for a reason.

It works!

Some believe Tarot cards are magical and possess some kind of supernatural power. Personally, I don't believe that. To me, they are coloured pieces of card which are mass-produced on a printing press, probably in China. Not very – woo, woo, I know! And yet, in time you will come to cherish your cards dearly – not for what they *are*, but for what they can *do*.

The Tarot, you see, is a bridge. It is a communication tool which connects you to a greater intelligence. Call that intelligence whatever you like – God, angels, spirit guides or universal consciousness. For the sake of a name for this book, I will call it 'The Universe'.

The Universe wants to communicate with you and provide answers to your questions. It wants to point you in the direction of whatever brings you the greatest sense of happiness and personal achievement. Normally, we experience this guidance in the form of hunches or gut feelings, which – depending on your level of sensitivity – can be difficult to interpret. The Tarot offers a solution. It acts as a boost, helping you to hear the Universe in a revolutionary, clear, and direct way.

Card Meanings

Traditionally, each Tarot card has a number of different meanings. This can sometimes be confusing. To avoid this, I have simplified matters by radically condensing the meaning of each card.

In case you think that refining the number of meanings is going to restrict your communication, please don't worry – you will find that it takes a lot of the guesswork out of your readings and provides clearer guidance. I recommend you *avoid* mixing meanings from different Tarot books; stick to the meanings I provide in this book. Make it your bible.

Understanding Spreads

If you have ever been to a Tarot reader, you will be familiar with the way in which they lay lots of cards out on the table in front of you. The pattern in which they lay the cards is called a *spread*.

A spread can consist of one card, or it can have up to 78 cards (the total number of cards in a Tarot deck). For example, the Celtic Cross spread (below) consists of 10 cards laid out in the shape of a cross.

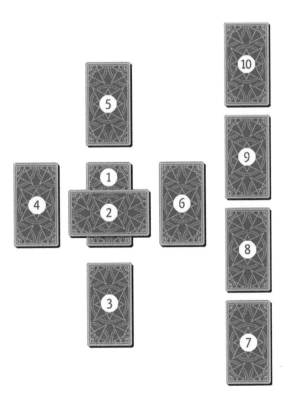

1: Your question

2: What supports or hinders you

3: Hidden influences

4: What happened in the recent past

5: What happens next

6: What happens in the near future

7: How you feel about the situation

8: What others think about you

9: Action you are advised to take

10: Outcome

Each position in a spread has a specific meaning, and this helps the reader to interpret the cards in a deeper way. As you become experienced in Tarot, you may want to learn more about spreads, and I include a few simple 3-card spreads at the back of the book.

However, I encourage you, for now, to stick to the one-card spread. The reason for this, is that you are looking for clarity – and one card leaves less wiggle room for misinterpretation. You ask a question, and draw a card. If you need clarification, you ask for clarification, and then draw another card. You can keep going as long as you like … do you see?

I have read Tarot cards for thousands of people and gradually, over time, I noticed that I was using spreads with fewer and fewer cards until, ultimately, I had it pared down to one card. Don't be fooled by the simplicity of the one-card spread. When you phrase your questions correctly, (and I will teach you how to do this), then the one-card spread is incredibly powerful and insightful. It is one of the best ways to master Tarot.

Section 2. Get To Know The Cards | Time: 2 Minutes

Different Types of Tarot Cards

There are 78 cards in a Tarot deck: 22 Major Arcana and 56 Minor Arcana. The word Arcana means 'secret', which gives a clue to the knowledge you are about to unlock. Major Arcana cards turn up when the Universe wants to talk about big events in your life, like marriage, major career changes, or moving location. Minor cards turn up when it wants to respond to day-to-day issues like *Will my meeting go well?* or *Will that guy I met last night send me a text?*

The Major Arcana

The Major Arcana refer to big events in your life, like marriage, the birth of a child, employment changes, and so on. Major Arcana are destiny cards so pay attention when one turns up in response to your question. It means that whatever happens next is destined. There is nothing you can do to change or influence the outcome. Fate has led you to this point and now you must go with the flow. Whatever occurs may be exciting or challenging, but either way, it always leads to something new and meaningful.

There are 22 Major Arcana cards, numbered 0 to 21. The first card is The Fool (0) and the last card is The World (21). You can think of these cards as a typical journey through life; we start off optimistic and foolish and eventually learn about the world through our experiences. If you lay all 22 cards out in front of you, you will see how the cards reflect the trials and tribulations of a typical life.

The Minor Arcana

The Minor Arcana refer to smaller, day-to-day events in your life like, *will my trip go well* or *will I hear back from so and so?* Unlike the Major Arcana, the Minor Arcana are not destiny cards. This means you are not necessarily beholden to the future they predict.

When you receive a Minor card in response to your question, it gives you a glimpse of the future according to the path you are on. If you are not happy with what you see, then ask the Tarot, *is there anything I can do to change the outcome?* Then draw another card for an answer. You may be guided to act in a different way or adopt a different attitude. Therein lies the true power of Tarot. Use the cards to shape the future you want!

Example Question

Will I do well in my interview tomorrow?

Card: 3 of Swords

Means: Disappointment! Oops!

Next Question

Is there anything I can do to improve my chances?

Card: 6 of Wands

Means: Victory!

Yes, you can turn this situation into a victory. When you read the deeper meaning of the 6 of Wands, it tells you "This is not a time for modesty or down-playing your abilities." In other words, the job is yours if you act like it is!

Notice, there are lots more Minor cards in the Tarot deck than Major cards. This tells us that destiny plays a smaller role in our lives than you may think. Mostly, we are free agents to do what we will with our life.

The Suits: Cups, Wands, Pentacles, and Swords

The Minor Arcana are divided into four suits: Wands, Cups, Swords, and Pentacles. Each suit has a characteristic which you should remember. Cups, for example, tend to refer to emotions. So, when a cup card turns up, you might think *Oh this is something to do with emotions*. Pentacles tend to refer to money and possessions, so when a pentacle turns up, you'll think *Oh, this is something to do with finances*.

Wands represent action. Wands are associated with positivity and a can-do attitude.

Example: Ace of Wands, suggests you embrace a new project!

Cups represent emotions. Cups are associated with water which symbolises our inner feelings. Love and passion are connected with Cups.

Example: Ace of Cups, you become passionate about a person or about something you are doing.

Swords represent thoughts. Swords are associated with the mind – what ideas you have and how you express them.

Example: Ace of Swords, you could be inspired by a new idea, and communicate it through writing, public speaking or the arts.

Pentacles represent practical matters. Pentacles are associated with money, property, work, study, and health – the practical things in life.

Example: Ace of Pentacles, you could start a new job or buy a house.

In all cases, the exact meaning will depend on the question you ask before drawing a card. If, for example, you drew the Ace of Cups and you had asked about love, then yes, you will find love soon. However, if you had asked about finding more meaningful employment, then it means you will find something you are passionate about doing. So, you see, it is important to be clear about your question before drawing a card. More about how to phrase a question, next …

Section 3. How To Ask A Question | Time: 1 Minute

1. Always Ask a Clear Question

Be certain you have a clear question before shuffling the cards. Jumbled thoughts produce jumbled results.

DON'T ASK: *Will I enjoy nursing or hairdressing?*

WHY NOT? Because you won't know whether the answer you receive refers to nursing or hairdressing.

INSTEAD ASK: *Will I enjoy nursing?*

Draw a card for a response. Then, return the card to the deck and shuffle again.

Then ask, *will I enjoy hairdressing?*

Always remember you are communicating with someone 'out there' in the Universe. Make it as easy as possible for the Universe to answer you clearly. The Universe only has 78 cards to reply to you with, so you must play your part by asking questions in a focused manner.

2. Don't Ask 'Should' I Do Something?

It is not someone else's job to make your mind up for you; after all, we have been granted free-will for a reason. Your journey in life is to learn to know yourself, and you should never give that power away. Questions which begin with 'Should I', rarely receive a clear response from the Tarot for this reason.

DON'T ASK: *Should I study nursing?*

INSTEAD ASK: *How will things turn out if I study nursing?*

Then, armed with the guidance you receive, you can easily make your decision.

3. One Card, One Question

When you ask a question, one card is usually enough to provide an answer. The more complicated the spread, the more possibilities for misinterpretation. At the back of this book, I include a couple of advanced spreads for the sake of variety, but I find – even as a highly experienced reader – that the *one question, one card* method is dependable because it leaves little room for misinterpretation.

Example: If you want to know about your future love life, you might ask 3 separate questions:

1. Will I find love?
2. Will we marry?
3. Will we have children?

Section 4. How To Perform A Reading | Time: 1 Minute

PLEASE NOTE: It is important that you stick to the following method exactly. Why? Because the Universe needs to know your intention before you start shuffling. How else can it ensure that the right card is on top when you stop shuffling? It needs to know the plan! The biggest mistake Tarot readers make is shuffling cards without communicating to the Universe, in advance, how they intend to pick a card. No wonder they end up with confusing results!

Here is my preferred method for performing a Tarot reading:

Method

Step 1

Ask a clear question. Ideally, write it down so there is no confusion.

Step 2

Rap the cards three times with your knuckles, or tap them three times on a surface like a table. This clears the energy.

Step 3

Shuffle the cards as you count to 10. I usually count, one hundred, two hundred, three hundred … and so on until ten hundred.

Step 4

Stop on ten and take the top card. This is your answer.

If a card flies out while you are shuffling, then accept that card as your answer. If more than one card flies out, put the cards back and start the process over again.

Questions & Answers

What happens if I do not receive a clear answer?

Occasionally, no matter how many times you ask a question, the Tarot may stubbornly refuse to provide an answer. In this case, accept that you are not meant to know at this time.

Do not ask, if you don't want to know!

Like a good friend, the cards will be honest, so only ask a question if you are ready to hear the truth.

What about timing? How will I know when something will happen?

Timing in Tarot can change slightly, as our actions can affect outcomes, particularly when it comes to Minor Cards. For that reason, I advise you not to become too obsessed about the 'when'. Go with the flow. That said, as a general rule, you should find that events unfold within 12 months.

Are some people harder to read than others?

Yes, but usually because they come to a reading with a closed mind. Maybe they sit with their arms folded and adopt a 'prove it to me' attitude which subconsciously creates a block. It's a shame because they are usually the ones who need the guidance the most. Other people can clam up if they do not hear what they want to hear, and this causes them to become resistant. Finally, personality plays a factor. If you do not like the person you are reading for, it is harder to connect. We are only human.

Is it unlucky to buy my own Tarot cards?

Where this notion originated from, I have no idea, but I am asked this question a lot. No, it is not unlucky. It makes no difference who buys your cards. I bought my own Rider-Waite deck! Frankly, I think it nice to pick the deck which will be your companion for years to come.

What is the best way to store my cards?

For many years, I wrapped my cards in a silk scarf or carried them in a velvet pouch. Nowadays, I keep them in a pretty wooden box. My cards are my treasure, and every time I open the box, it reminds me something magical is about to happen. There is no right or wrong way to store Tarot cards, but in time you will instinctively feel a need to protect them from outside influences. In the beginning, I used to allow people to touch my cards, but I don't allow this any longer. You may find that your Tarot cards become so sensitive and attuned to your energy, that it feels almost physically uncomfortable when someone else handles them.

Congratulations, you have finished your Tarot course! Now you are ready to ask your first question and receive some star-studded universal guidance.

Welcome to Team Tarot.

Love

Karina

TAROT CARD MEANINGS

MAJOR ARCANA

The Fool (0): Exciting New Beginning

Key Meaning: The Fool signifies an exciting new beginning.

The Card: A carefree young man carrying a satchel is about to step off a cliff as he looks up at the sun. His little dog dances at his feet, as happy-go-lucky as he is. When the Fool appears, it means your life is about to change in an unexpected but wonderful way. Be prepared to lighten your load and junk old ideas, routines, and even spiritual beliefs. What has gone before may have served you well, but it is time for a transformation. Most likely, you are ready for this, even enthusiastic about the idea! The number on the Fool card is zero, which represents the moment before the Big Bang and creation. Currently, anything is possible, all possibilities exist. What occurs now is likely to come out of the blue. You could end up starting a new business, job, or course; move location or begin a relationship. Yet, this is only the beginning, the first step of a grander adventure to come. The only thing you need do is embrace what occurs, with trust in your heart. Take a leap of faith. The Universe is about to open its doors, and it is time to rediscover your youthful optimism and step through.

Karina Says: Free your spirit. Free yourself to love, travel, think, or work in a way which satisfies you at a soul level. There are no guarantees in life, so do not waste time waiting for one.

Other Possible Meanings

- If you asked, should I move country? The answer is yes.
- If you asked, should I pursue this relationship? Yes, take a risk.
- If you are focused on your spiritual development, trust the ideas which come to you now. Higher powers are encouraging you to think (and act) out of the box.

Meanings When Reversed

Upside down the sun is setting, and the young man lands on his head. This indicates you are rushing too quickly into a situation, ignoring the advice of others or your inner voice. Be careful, or you may set yourself up for a nasty fall.

Alternatively, you may feel stuck, and lacking motivation or courage to try new things. Draw another card for guidance on how to overcome this block.

The Magician (1): Make It Happen!

Key Meaning: The Magician signifies that now is the time to follow through on your idea. Make it happen!

The Card: The Magician points a wand up towards heaven, and a hand down towards the earth. This signifies you can channel magical powers from above and turn your dreams into something concrete and real. The world is ready to receive what you are about to say or do. The number on the Magician card is 1, representing the first step of creation. Have confidence; you are more than prepared for this next phase in your life; the time is right. Notice that all the elements of the Tarot are on the table ready for your use: the wand (enthusiasm), cup (creativity), pentacle (resources) and sword (ideas). You have all the tools necessary to see this through. Whatever lifestyle you want to create, however unique your vision or message, you can make it happen. You are the powerful Magician, with manifestation tricks at your fingertips.

Karina Says: Raise your eyes towards the heavens and ask: *How can I be of service?*

Other Possible Meanings

- This message is only if you have already shown a serious interest in magical arts. You have a natural talent for mediumship, good enough in fact to become a professional! At the very least, you display an extraordinary talent for channelling important information from the other side.
- Now is the time to complete that lingering, half-finished project. Finish it and promote it.
- If you asked about fertility: Yes, you can conceive a baby.

Meanings When Reversed

Upside down, the tools fall off the Magician's table. This means your thoughts are scattered, and there is a risk you could miss an opportunity.

- Focus and put more effort into your idea, study, or project.
- You lack confidence in yourself or your idea. You should not!

The High Priestess (2):
Listen To Your Intuition

II The High Priestess

Key Meaning: The High Priestess signifies you should listen to your intuition.

The Card: The High Priestess sits on her throne, a mystical figure and bearer of ancient knowledge. A half-hidden scroll on her lap represents the mysteries and secrets of life. The crescent moon at her feet and on her crown represents psychic intuition. When this card appears, and you have an important decision to make, it means you should follow your gut instinct. Place more importance on what you *feel* like doing, rather than what you *ought* to do. This is because higher powers are feeding you guidance through your senses rather than logical mind. The High Priestess often appears when we begin to ask the big questions like *Why am I here* and *What is my purpose?* Know that you are on the correct path to uncovering these secrets and so much more. You are experiencing an exciting awakening, and the High Priestess advises you to prepare for dramatic changes in your life or work, possibly starting as soon as the next new moon.

Karina Says: Be alert to signs from the spirit world, they are letting you know that they are listening and helping you behind the scenes. Their sign could be anything: a cold breeze, a feather dropping from the sky, items going missing, a bird pecking at your window, whatever makes you think 'Oh, that's strange.'

Other Possible Meanings

- If you asked about spiritual work or study, the answer is YES. Go ahead and immerse yourself. Ancient knowledge is available to you now and comes as a speedy download. You are remembering rather than learning for the first time.
- If you asked about a medical issue, consider having your hormone levels checked.

Meanings When Reversed

Reversed, the High Priestess falls off her throne and becomes disorientated and less certain of herself.

- Either you are ignoring your intuition or have problems accessing it. Draw another card for guidance on what to do.

The Empress (3): A Creative Explosion

Key Meaning: The Empress signifies a big creative explosion which transforms your life.

The Card: The Empress is the mother of all that grows; she is a fertile force of ideas and productivity. She sits on her throne surrounded by a luscious countryside. Her crown sparkles with the 12 stars of the zodiac and her shield is marked by the symbol of Venus, the planet of love. When the Empress appears, it is a wonderful sign for your future! You are in the process of giving birth to something hugely important. Depending on your circumstances, this literally could mean the birth of a child. However, it could also herald the explosion of a creative project, job, business, or love affair which magically transforms your life. You are entering a time of great fortune and abundance, so have faith and throw your heart and soul into whatever presents next. As a Major Arcana card, the Empress reminds you, this is your destiny.

Karina Says: The Empress is a powerful symbol of femininity, the gentler side of human nature. What or who is it you wish to nurture at this time? Be filled by this purpose and throw yourself into it.

Other Possible Meanings

- If you asked can I conceive a healthy child? The answer is yes.
- If you asked about a house move or home renovation, then yes, it will happen.
- If you asked about a new relationship, then yes this relationship will blossom.

Meanings When Reversed

When the Empress is reversed, she struggles to remain in control of her environment.

- Are you neglecting to take care of yourself? Give yourself permission to put yourself first.
- If you are experiencing problems becoming pregnant, draw another card for guidance on what action to take.

The Emperor (4):
Deal With The Problem

Key Meaning: The Emperor signifies that it is time to deal with a problem that has been holding you back.

The Card: The Emperor sits on his throne, wearing a suit of armour. Everything about this card suggests power and authority. He is ready to do battle for what he wants. When this card appears, it means you should not wait for *life* or a stroke of good luck to shape the future you want. While you will be blessed with much fortune ahead, right now you need to step up, make plans, and work towards your goals. How else can you grow as a person and be proud of your success? You must occupy the driving seat of this Ferrari which is your life. Fortunately, the Universe is sending you a blast of courage and motivation so that you can set in motion what needs to happen. Make the most of this powerful time to enact changes in your career, study life, personal projects or relationships – wherever it is you wish for 'more' in your life. Please note, the Emperor only appears to those for whom Destiny has great plans. So, rest assured, the path ahead is bright and wonderful.

Karina Says: Become the Emperor by dealing with your worries head-on. It is an illusion that we can hide from our problems, they remain in the background, lurking and dragging us down.

Other Possible Meanings

- If you apply for a job in a large institution or corporation, you are successful.
- If you are struggling with authorities and red tape, be patient and follow the rules. All will turn out well.
- If you asked about your life purpose, consider teaching or counselling.
- If you asked about a man, know that he is reliable, honest, and supportive. (If the card is reversed, the opposite is true.)

Meanings When Reversed

Upside down, the Emperor falls from his throne and loses his courage.

- You feel intimidated in the face of competition or adversity. Dig deep and discover your fighting spirit. It is there, I promise!

Hierophant (5): Be A Leader!

Key Meaning: The Hierophant signifies that you have what it takes to lead and inspire others.

The Card: The Hierophant (or Pope) sits on his throne, dispensing advice to his priests. The keys at the Hierophant's feet represent the keys to the Kingdom of Heaven. As such, his role is to act as a bridge between Heaven and Earth, passing on the wisdom he receives. When this card appears, it means you are ready to adopt a leadership role, perhaps at work or in the community. You may welcome this guidance (or fight it), but regardless, now is the time to act. Higher powers wish to put your abilities to better use and, in so doing, you gain the respect of others. This may mean organising an event, teaching, public speaking, or passing on knowledge in some way. In order to do this, you must emerge from behind the computer screen or home, wherever it is you have been hiding. Centre stage no less! When the Hierophant appears, you may also feel a need to find a deeper meaning to life, to explore spiritual matters. If you are looking for a spiritual mentor to take you to the next level, one should appear shortly.

Karina Says: A beautiful mind is all it takes to inspire others.

Other Possible Meanings

- Your relationship develops to the next level. I hear wedding bells!
- If you are looking for a conventional job within a large institution or local company, you are successful in your search.
- You find spiritual guidance within traditional religion or by studying in a group setting.

Meanings When Reversed

Even reversed, the Hierophant is still positive. He heralds escape from conventionality. Perhaps you quit a dull job and decide to follow your dreams. Or maybe you stop worrying about what others think about you, and this frees you to express yourself in exciting new ways. Sometimes, a reversal indicates leaving behind your traditional religious upbringing and choosing to look at the world in a different way.

The Lovers (6): A New Passion

Key Meaning: The Lovers signify a new passion. Either you are about to fall in love, or you discover a love for what you are doing.

The Card: A naked man and woman stand beneath Archangel Raphael. This is Adam and Eve in the Garden of Eden. Behind the couple is the Tree of Knowledge, representing an awakening; a growing awareness of what is important in life. When this card appears, it means you are about to fall in love. Someone enters your life, and this is the romance of a lifetime, leading to a blissful marriage. If you are not looking for love, this passion can come in another form. It may be discovering the love of a new business, hobby, or career. There is an element of choice with The Lovers, so your new passion may require you to make a brave decision. It is possible that you could run from what is on offer and play it safe. Or, you could take a chance on life. As the Lovers is a Major Arcana card, it means that whatever you decide now will alter the course of your destiny.

Karina Says: A life without passion is not living, it is merely existing. Trust the feeling welling up inside you; the one which calls you to act.

Other Possible Meanings

- If you asked 'Is this the correct path for me?' the answer is yes.
- If you are a student of spiritual matters, higher powers are calling on you to be of greater service. Draw another card for guidance on your next step.

Meanings When Reversed

When reversed, the mountains in the background suddenly appear more prominent and divide the lovers. This means there are obstacles in your way.

- If you started a new relationship, it has difficulties getting off the ground. Are you making poor choices in love? Draw another card for an answer.
- If you are doing something you love but experiencing problems in attaining results, draw another card for guidance. Ask the Tarot, what do I need to do next?

The Chariot (7): Triumph After Hardship

VII The Chariot

Key Meaning: The Chariot signifies triumph after hardship. The worst is behind you, and the future is brighter.

The Card: A valiant Prince steers his chariot proudly through the streets. He is sheltered under a canopy decorated with the stars of celestial guidance. Notice that the chariot has no reigns, which means he has disciplined the sphinxes through sheer willpower. When this card appears, it means *where* there has been stagnation or lack of progress in your life, there is now movement. The black and white sphinxes represent opposing forces, so whatever it is you had to 'hold together', in order to reach this point, you have now mastered and become stronger for it. The Universe rewards you and the stars smile upon you. You are magnetic to others, appearing strong and capable. Right now, you can attract whatever you seek: career success, public recognition, rewards, or prizes. As the Chariot is a Major Arcana card, it indicates that the journey it took to get here was all part of a larger plan called *your destiny*.

Karina Says: It is easy to have faith when we are not tested. Real faith is the ability to keep going, even when we cannot see the light, but you know – in your heart – it is there.

Other Possible Meanings

- If you asked: Will I be traveling soon, or travelling for work? Yes, you will.
- If you asked: Will I buy a car soon? Yes, you will.
- If you asked: Am I on the right path or do I have the strength to keep going? The answer is yes.

Meanings When Reversed

Reversed, our brave Prince lands on his head, causing everything to come to a standstill. A reversal is still good; it just indicates a delay.

- If you are planning a trip or making travel arrangements, be prepared for problems or delays.
- Are you finding it difficult to stick to your goals? Don't worry; tomorrow is another day. The chariot will move forward again as you regain your motivation.

Strength (8): Conquer Your Fears

Key Meaning: The Strength card indicates now is the time for you to conquer your fears. Do the thing you fear, and success and happiness will be your ultimate reward.

The Card: A woman closes a lion's mouth in a gentle, yet firm way. The lion represents our fears and the scary thoughts which stop us from doing things. This card is a reminder to draw on your well of inner strength to overcome self-doubt and fear. Have faith that you are strong, and you will not let yourself down. When you free yourself of fear, you can do more with your life. Deal with conflict and struggle (including inner struggle) in a gentle but firm way. For example, speak up and say what is on your mind with a smile; do not wait until you blow up in anger. Be calm but persistent until others give way to your needs. Draw on feminine qualities to get your way – charm and diplomacy. When this card appears, it means you have all the strength and skills you need to achieve what you want; you just needed reminding. You are not a victim of circumstances; you are a majestic warrior! As a Major Arcana card, it is your destiny to step into your personal power and amaze us all.

Karina Says: When you are not sure what you want, then flip a coin. When that coin is in the air, you will quickly realise which way you want it to fall.

Other Possible Meanings

- If you asked: Will my health improve? The strength card is the most important card in Tarot for self-healing. You have the ability to draw on divine superpowers of healing through meditation and faith to bring about a full recovery. The more you believe this, the faster the recovery.

- If you asked: Should I pursue a healing career? It is your destiny to bring healing to the world, and you must act now. Time is running out for humanity.

- You asked about love: At this time, you are blooming and oozing sex appeal. Have confidence in yourself to attract the perfect partner, or to seduce the one you have!

Meanings When Reversed

Reversed, the lion is suddenly in control. This means you are allowing fear or other people to prevent you from doing or saying what you want. Stop! Calm the lion and face your fears. In the process, you will discover that the lion is really a pussycat and that your thoughts are far worse than the reality!

The Hermit (9): Spend Time Alone

Key Meaning: The Hermit signifies you should spend time alone to gather your thoughts about life and the future.

The Card: The Hermit stands alone on a snowy mountaintop, holding a lantern to illuminate the path ahead. A hermit is someone who chooses to spend time apart from others, either because he is tired of their company or he wants to contemplate life in the hope of finding enlightenment. We all need time alone, not because we are anti-social, but because it is the only way to quieten our minds and sort out our thoughts. As soon as you start to ask 'Who am I?' or 'Where is my life going?', you have reached the Hermit stage! The Hermit is represented by the number 9, considered the end of a cycle in numerology. This is a time to reflect and boost your spiritual connection before a new era begins. This period cannot be rushed, but requires me-time, meditation, journaling, and prayer. What you uncover or learn about yourself is truly wonderful and energises you for adventures ahead. As the Hermit is a Major Arcana card, it means whatever time you take for yourself, now, is not a luxury but a necessity.

Karina Says: We cannot hear our own thoughts in this noisy world without escaping to a private space. The Dalai Lama urges us to 'spend some time alone every day.'

Other Possible Meanings

- You may meet an important guru now, but consider perhaps you are also emerging as the guru?
- You are comfortable being alone and do not feel lonely. This is because you are an evolved soul who needs fewer distractions than younger souls.
- If you asked: Would I benefit from counselling? The answer is yes.

Meanings When Reversed

Reversed, the lamp falls out of the Hermit's hand, and he is alone in the dark.

Are you afraid of being by yourself? Being alone is not the same as loneliness. Real loneliness is distressing because it means you have difficulties bonding with other people. If you feel you have problems relating to people, then draw another card for guidance on how best to help yourself. However, choosing to be alone or socialising less because you want to focus on other elements of your life – like a job, study, project, or spiritual development – is different. Sometimes, it is necessary to withdraw in order to achieve what we must.

The Wheel of Fortune (10): Lucky You!

Key Meaning: The Wheel of Fortune signifies an amazing period of good luck coming your way. Lucky You!

The Card: Congratulations, you drew the luckiest card in the Tarot deck! The wheel in this card represents the passage of time and the changing patterns of our lives. Luck comes and goes; sometimes we are happy, and sometimes we are sad. It is the cycle of life: up and down. The good news is, the wheel has spun in your favour, and you are entering an extremely lucky period in your life. Good luck, unexpected opportunities, a lottery win, travel, career possibilities – anything is possible. The Wheel of Fortune is a destiny card, which means whatever happens now *feels* like destiny or synchronicity, rather than coincidence. Perhaps you even sense 'It is my time, I deserve a break.' Notice there are no humans pictured in this Tarot card – there are four fixed signs of the zodiac (representing air, earth, fire and water) and mythical creatures – but no people. This is to demonstrate that a higher power than mankind is at work. There is nothing you need do to trigger this good fortune; fate is already in motion.

Karina Says: After bad luck comes good fortune. (An old gypsy proverb.)

Other Possible Meanings

- If you asked the question – should I go for it? The answer is yes!

Meanings When Reversed

Reversed, the wheel turns in the opposite direction, indicating a less lucky period. Timing is everything. Be patient; the wheel will inevitably change again.

- This is not a good time to take a big risk or gamble on risky investments.

- A situation is not ripe enough to act on yet. Making a move would be premature.

Justice (11): Be Logical!

Key Meaning: Justice signifies you should be logical and less emotional at this time.

The Card: Lady Justice holds a scale in one hand and a sword pointing towards heaven in the other. She reminds us that all the things we do and say – both good and bad – are recorded in the Akashic records, and we will be judged. We receive our *just* rewards; what goes around, comes around. This card often appears when we have a decision to make, and we are urged to choose the moral path and do the right thing. This situation may involve a friendship, relationship, or family matter. Try to keep your emotions in check and do not act or speak on impulse. Pretend you are a judge, reviewing your case impartially. What logically is the best solution for all involved? The Justice card also appears when we are at a crossroads in life, trying to figure out our future plans – such as where to live, how to live, or what to do for a living. The guidance of this card is to strip away illusions. Be realistic rather than idealistic. Ask yourself, what is more sensible right now? Destiny has brought you to this crossroads for a reason; a new approach is necessary. It may be boring to act logically but, in so doing, you will reap the rewards in years to come.

Karina Says: Life can make us bitter, or it can make us more determined to leave the world a better place than we found it. It is your choice as to which path you choose.

Other Possible Meanings

- If you are involved in a court case, there is a decision in your favour.
- If someone has wrongly accused you, an apology will be forthcoming.
- If you asked about a career, consider law, law enforcement, or a job where you can solve the injustices of the world.

Meanings When Reversed

Reversed, the scale falls out of Lady Justice's hand. This means you are not being dealt a fair hand.

- If you are involved in, or considering taking a court case, there will be delays.
- Do you feel there is an imbalance in your life? Are you giving too much – perhaps in a relationship, friendship, or job – and not receiving enough in return?

In both instances, draw another card to see what action you can take, if any, to reverse the unfairness of your situation at this time. Remember, the righteous always receive justice in the end.

The Hanged Man (12): Do Nothing!

Key Meaning: The Hanged Man signifies you should hold fire and do nothing for now.

The Card: A man hangs from a tree; one foot raised in a yoga pose. He is not in any danger; in fact, he looks peaceful in his meditative state. Around his head is a halo of light which represents enlightenment and connection to higher powers. When the Hanged Man appears, it means you are in a state of limbo. Things cannot go back to the way they were, nor can you move forward yet. This period could be frustrating unless you see it for what it is: a pause to reflect and deepen your spirituality. As a major destiny card, the Hanged Man guides you to slow down and connect with your true purpose. This card often appears when a person is ready to take their spirituality more seriously: to study, meditate and write. You may even be moving from student to guru status as natural abilities emerge. It also appears when we are going through a major transition period, transitioning from one way of living to another, one value system to another. Expect a new direction to emerge over the coming months, perhaps even a complete reversal of lifestyle.

Karina Says: The next phase of your life will require a different version of you. Reach deep inside.

Other Possible Meanings

- If you asked about a problem, the solution will appear when you take a break and come back to it with fresh eyes.
- If you asked *when* will a particular thing happen – the answer is not soon. There may be delays and frustrations, but trust that everything is working out as it should.
- If you experienced an unpleasant event recently, like the breakup of a relationship, illness, job loss, or business disappointment, try not to worry. Take time to reflect on what happened. What you discover about yourself, and what you want from life, may be radically changing.

Meanings When Reversed

When the Hanged Man is reversed, he is released from his binds and jumps free. The waiting period is over, and now you can move forward!

- Events you are waiting on, or hoping for, will soon take place.
- You have all the spiritual guidance you need to act. Do not worry about outcomes or what people will think of you.

Death (13): The End - Time To Move On

Key Meaning: Death signifies the end of a chapter in your life; it is time to move on.

The Card: The Grim Reaper rides his horse towards a bishop, a child, and a woman. The king lies dead in the background, his crown knocked off, indicating that the old ways have been overthrown. The Reaper carries a banner with a picture of a rose, a symbol of change and rebirth. Notice that while destruction is all around, the rising sun and the defiant bishop seem to offer the promise of a new dawn. Death does not predict an actual death, but rather the end of a way of life. When Death turns up, it means that the question on your mind when you shuffled the cards has already been decided; whatever it is – whether a relationship, job, or situation – it is at an end. It is over and done with; there is nothing you can do to alter the outcome. This may be cause for celebration if you are waiting for an end to a situation. Alternatively, it may leave you feeling sad if you are not ready to let go and move on. Death says there is no going back. At this point, you may not know what the future holds, but trust that new opportunities are already in the process of emerging. This is a moment of transition and rebirth.

Karina Says: Stay calm if life takes an unexpected twist. The Universe has an alternative plan in mind for you.

Other Possible Meanings

- Are you fascinated with life-after-death, spirituality, shamanism, or the magical realm? You are curious for a reason; it is not a coincidence. Dig deep and learn all you can.
- If you have been trying to kick a habit or lose weight, this time you are successful once and for all.

Meanings When Reversed

When Death is reversed, the horse ends up on his back, and no movement is possible.

- Are you resisting change? There is no sense in putting off the inevitable; it only wastes time. Know when to let go and allow better things to come.
- If you are waiting for a situation to come to an end, there are likely to be delays.

Temperance (14): You Are Healed

XIV Temperance

Key Meaning: Temperance signifies you are healing after a period of stress or ill health.

The Card: Archangel Michael pours water from one cup to another; a symbolic act of the cleansing and renewal of your energy. Notice he has one foot on land (representing your physical body) and one foot in water (your emotions). He is restoring balance to your body and mind. If you have been through a difficult time, this card predicts that more peaceful, happier days are approaching. There will be harmony in all areas of your life: relationships, family, finances, and health. Temperance is a truly magical card, and as a Major Arcana, it is as though you are being touched by an angel. When Temperance turns up, you are also likely to be mastering the art of patience. Learning how to stick to something without giving up too easily. Or learning to go with the flow and accepting that not everything can happen the moment we want it to. In a way, you are discovering the power of faith.

Karina Says: Patience is not about doing nothing. It is *all* about *doing* but being patient about the results.

Other Possible Meanings

- If you asked about choosing a career, consider anything in the healing arts or something which makes the world a more beautiful or kinder place.
- If you asked about your health, consider cleaning up your diet. Temperance is the card of moderation and balance.

Meanings When Reversed

When Temperance is reversed, Archangel Michael struggles to complete his work.

- Are you being impatient? Do you tend to give up too easily? The same sort of problems will crop up – again and again – until you master patience.
- Have you overindulged or been unable to give your body the love it needs recently? Now is a perfect time to get back into shape.

The Devil (15): Free Yourself

Key Meaning: The Devil indicates you should free yourself from an unhealthy situation.

The Card: The Devil clings with clawed feet to a bare rock. The reversed star on his head indicates the lack of Light and happiness. A naked couple are chained to the rock, seemingly at the monster's mercy. When the Devil appears, take note. It means you risk making a choice which could harm you. Or, perhaps you are already knee-deep in a situation, mindset, or lifestyle which is not fulfilling, but from which you find it difficult to escape. The Devil is a Major Arcana card, which means he speaks of important issues. If you do something now to change your direction, you will transform your future and increase your happiness tenfold. Although you may not realise it, you are standing at an important juncture in life. Will you break free from the chains that hold you back? Whether those chains are real, or in your mind, they are limiting your beautiful life. Notice how the chains around the couple's necks are loose; they are not as enslaved as they think. All it requires is some courage and a desire for more. You have the power to change direction and make your life a whole lot better.

Karina Says: When we dance too long with the Devil, he does not change. But he does change us.

Other Possible Meanings

Are you:

- Holding on to hurt and anger? Free yourself. Move on emotionally.
- Obsessed by an ex-? Free yourself.
- Prone to feeling negative? Free yourself.
- Over-eating, gambling, drinking too much, or smoking? Free yourself.
- Holding back because you worry what people will think of you? Free yourself.
- Tied to an abusive, selfish, or unfaithful partner? Free yourself.
- Bored by your job or daily life? Free yourself.

If you need guidance on how to free yourself, draw another card and ask 'What is my first step?'

Meanings When Reversed

Reversed, the couple cast off their chains and are back in control. This means you are in the process of freeing yourself from whatever or whoever has held you back.

The Tower (16): Bolt From The Blue

Key Meaning: The Tower indicates a bolt from the blue, an unexpected event which forces change.

The Card: The Tower is one of the *change* cards in Tarot but, in this case, change is sudden and not necessarily welcome. A bolt of lightning hits a tower, setting it on fire and tossing the king and queen out of their home. The symbolism here is similar to the Garden of Eden; a couple banished by the hand of God. When this card appears, it means fate has, or soon will, intervene to force change which you know in your heart is overdue. Ultimately, what transpires sends you in a new direction, hurling you towards your true destiny. The Tower strips away any false sense of security, in your home, relationships, work, belief system, or sense of self. It may even feel like the Universe is 'out to get you' as events come with speed, one thing after the other. The problems cannot be dodged but must be faced and dealt with. At first, you may resist, but then you become excited as you start to see the potential of what is unfolding before you. Higher powers are protecting you, stretching you, directing you towards a situation more amazing than you could ever have dreamed of.

Karina Says: Everything is falling apart and coming together at the same time.

Other Possible Meanings

- If you asked about property, check for construction problems. When I received the Tower, my apartment *literally* collapsed (it turns out the builders did not put in strong enough foundations).

- If you asked about world events, this card can herald a sudden event like a natural disaster, unexpected change of government, or terrorist attack.

Meanings When Reversed

Reversed, the king and queen appear to fall in slow motion. This means events are crumbling around you more slowly, giving you time to prepare for change. Make use of the time!

- Do you have the gift of premonition? The Tower reversed is like 'seeing' the future, in slow motion, before it happens.

The Star (17): Your Wish Comes True

XVII The Star

Key Meaning: The Star indicates your wish comes true.

The Card: A naked woman kneels at the water's edge. She pours a jug of water over the land and another into a pool of water. The land represents your earthly practical needs like good health and money, and the pool represents your deep emotions. This watering is a symbol of revitalisation and cleansing; you are being renewed physically, emotionally, and spiritually. The Star is one of the luckiest cards in Tarot, and when it appears, it means your dream is about to come true. Lucky you! The Star is the ultimate healing card, and it shines light on your life where healing and good fortune is most needed. It usually appears after we have been through difficult times (which is why it appears numerically after the Devil and Tower cards). This is the same star of Bethlehem and the star which tops a fairy's wand. If you enjoy meditation, focus on this card for a quick feel-good boost. Simply relax, stare at the card, and repeat: All my dreams are coming true.

Karina Says: No matter what is happening in your life, never be afraid to hope and dream. People who stop dreaming have given up on life.

Other Possible Meanings

- Did you ask about health? The Star heralds healing, perhaps even a miracle! It reminds us never to give up hope.
- Did you ask, will I be famous or recognised for my talents? Yes, you have 'star' quality.
- If you are a stargazer and often wonder 'what's out there?' – consider studying astronomy, astrology, or even ufology!

Meanings When Reversed

When the Star is reversed, the light does not shine as brightly, and its healing powers are limited. This means you have a mental block which is limiting your life.

What is your block?

- Have you lost belief that things will get better?
- Do you struggle to value your beauty and talents? You are a star in waiting.
- Do you secretly feel that luck is for other people and not for you?

Turn the card the right way up! You received this message because now is the time to shake off those limiting beliefs. Allow the star to shine brightly on your life. All you need to do is reverse your thinking and say 'Yes, I believe good things can happen to me.' Repeat and repeat until you have cleansed your mind!

The Moon (18): You Are
Receiving Messages

Key Meaning: The Moon signifies you are receiving messages from the spirit world.

The Card: Two wolves howl at the moon, and a lobster climbs out of the water; is he friend or foe? The bright full moon casts shadows over the land, and not everything is as it seems. When the Moon appears, emotions are high; you feel confused and uncertain about your future. You sense the Universe is sending you signs, you experience synchronicity, it feels like something big is coming, but you do not know what. You may fluctuate wildly from 'It's all in my head' to 'I know.' When you receive the Moon card, it is a confirmation that you *are* receiving messages, although you may not fully understand the mechanics yet. Something big is coming; it could be a move, job change, an unexpected opportunity, a download of inspiration, or the emergence of a powerful gift ... anything. Just be patient, all will be revealed soon. If you receive the Moon card regularly, then it is a sign you should raise your sights beyond the mundane. You could feel at home on the astral plane, having out of body experiences, writing supernatural fiction, investigating UFOs, studying past life regression, or acting as a psychic or medium. Someone needs to educate the world. Why not you?

Karina Says: You have a creative mind and the ability to 'see' what others do not. More importantly, you can manifest what you see and turn it into something real.

Other Possible Meanings

- If you are psychic, your powers are intensifying, and you are able to tune into the collective consciousness. The knowledge you gain must be shared with others.
- If you asked about pregnancy or childbirth, the next full moon will deliver a result.

Meanings When Reversed

When reversed, the moon seems to become brighter, and the animals become calmer. This means, whatever knowledge was hidden, reveals itself now. You have all the insight you need to take action.

The Sun (19): Success

Key Meaning: The Sun represents success! An era of happiness, health, and wealth is approaching.

The Card: The blazing sun shines down on a healthy little boy and his horse. This is the happiest picture in the Tarot deck; it positively radiates joy. The red drape signifies energy and creativity, and the horse represents freedom, travel, and movement. When the Sun appears, you start attracting great fortune and success in all areas of your life. Your past efforts are rewarded, and present difficulties are overcome. The Sun represents a healthy body and mind. Healthy pregnancy. Success in exams, business, work, travel, creative pursuits, love, and marriage. Success in whatever you focused on when you drew this card. Higher powers are acknowledging it is time for your day in the sun. There is a sense of youthful optimism about you, and people even start commenting on how young you are looking. In a way, the Sun card is a form of graduation; you have done all the work, come full circle, and now you can claim your reward!

Karina Says: Keep your face to the sun, and you will never see the shadows (Helen Keller).

Other Possible Meanings

- If you asked about a child, do not worry. They will be healthy, happy, and successful.
- If you asked about a sun holiday or emigrating – yes, go for it and have fun!
- If you are worried about your health or test results, everything turns out well.

Meanings When Reversed

The sun shines less brightly when the card is reversed, and the horse cannot move so easily. This indicates delays. Success and happiness take a little longer to achieve. Often the delay is caused by an internal block; it may be that you are feeling depressed, burnt out, or suffering from low self-esteem. Now is the time to knock any problems on the head; reclaim your optimism. Draw another card for guidance if necessary.

Judgement (20): Cosmic Wake-Up Call

Key Meaning: Judgement signifies a cosmic wake-up call.

The Card: Archangel Gabriel blows his trumpet, waking people from their coffins and slumber. This may seem like a scary card, but Judgement predicts the resurrection – a wonderful surge of energy and motivation in your life. Sometimes, it appears when we have had a crisis which acted like a cosmic wake-up call. Judgement is the second-last card in the Major Arcana and comes just before a new dawn. When it appears, you may feel like you are seeing the world with fresh eyes; as though you are waking from a slumber. You begin to see solutions to problems which have evaded you in the past; worries evaporate and appear smaller on the scale of things after this new awakening. Suddenly, time is of the essence, and you feel an urge to move forward more bravely. You may feel drawn to a new hobby or job, or the need to express yourself and emerge from the shadows.

Karina Says: The world is waking up, and you are not alone in experiencing this shift. Take your place at the front of the queue and light the way for others.

Other Possible Meanings

- A situation, once considered dead, returns to life. It depends on what you focused on as you shuffled the cards. For example, an ex- returns, you receive a job offer from an old employer, or you move back to a place you lived before.
- If you asked, do I have psychic/mediumship abilities? Yes, you do! A gift can be dormant for years and then re-emerge out of the blue.

Meanings When Reversed

When Judgement is reversed, Gabriel blows his trumpet, but the people are disorientated and not listening.

- The Universe is trying to tell you something. If you are not sure what, draw another card for guidance.
- Are you hiding your talents for fear of what others will think of you? Or maybe you are not putting enough effort into your development? Are you fearful or superstitious? Whatever it is, wake up! Step into your power.

The World (21): The End and The Beginning

Key Meaning: The World indicates the end of a phase, and the beginning of a new one.

The Card: A naked maiden dances with joy as she takes her place in the centre of the world. As The World is the final Major Arcana card in Tarot, it celebrates your life, the ups and the downs, the knowledge you have gained about yourself, and the lessons you have learnt. Higher powers never expected you to be perfect, merely that you played your part and tried. When the World appears, it means you have done well, and it is time to move on to something new. A project or phase of your life is successfully completed. The four mythical creatures from the Wheel of Fortune card appear again to reassure you that the next phase of your life will be even more exciting and fortunate. You may, or may not, have plans at this stage; either way, do not worry. You have the skills and motivation now to be an even greater success, to take centre stage. You have arrived at a cosmic state of awareness, and there is a sense of liberation as old fears and limitations vanish. You are free to fly high as a bird.

Karina Says: There are times in life when we need to try harder, and there are times to walk away. This is time to walk away.

Other Possible Meanings

- If you asked about travel or emigration, yes, this is a good time to see more of the world.
- Did you ask about moving house? Yes, the Universe supports your idea.
- Keep your dreams alive – you have the ability to achieve your heart's desire.

Meanings When Reversed

When the World is reversed, the news is still good, but there are delays. The end is not quite in sight yet.

- Carry on as you are, things will work themselves out.
- Travel or moving plans are delayed.

MINOR CARDS

WANDS

Ace of Wands: A Fresh Start!

Ace of Wands

Key Meaning: The Ace of Wands indicates a fresh start. A new opportunity emerges which – if you embrace it with enthusiasm – promises to transform your life. Wands can relate to any part of your life: creative thoughts, spiritual pursuits, work, family, or health.

The Card: An illuminated hand emerges from the sky, offering you a wand. The wand symbolises a fresh start. Perhaps you have been hungry for adventure or searching for a new direction. This card indicates an exciting new opportunity brewing which brilliantly fulfils your needs. A specific opportunity may arrive, or it may be that you adopt a new attitude about a situation and approach it with renewed energy. Either way, the green shoots on the wand indicate that this is only the beginning. Like all Aces, this card represents potential. You still need to grab the wand and do something with it!

Karina Says: Trust your vision and believe that you can bring it to fruition. Cast doubt aside and focus your energy on *doing*. The Universe has opened a door, but it is still up to you to step through it.

Other Possible Meanings

- If you are wondering if your idea is worth pursuing … the answer is Yes!
- Now is the time to be led by passion, do not overthink the situation.

Meanings When Reversed

The Ace loses its power when reversed. This indicates delays or problems, but your idea is still worth pursuing.

- There are delays to plans. Draw another card for guidance on the cause of this delay.
- You lack the confidence to pursue your idea. Shame, because you could be brilliant.
- Someone lets you down. Don't give up, something better will turn up.

2 of Wands: Dream Big

Key Meaning: The 2 of Wands indicates it is safe to dream big. Whatever project you are working on now – whether personal or work related – it will blossom into something wonderful.

The Card: A man stands on the top of his castle looking out to sea. Beside him, fastened to the wall is the Ace of Wands which he has successfully managed to turn into the present situation. Now, he has a second wand; a sign that it is time to contemplate his next move. The globe in his hand expresses how he feels: 'The world is my oyster'. When this card appears, you are feeling positive and have moved beyond the initial stages of a project. Results begin to show, inspiring you to dream even bigger.

Karina Says: Fortune is on your side at this time, but you still need to play your part and remain focused.

Other Possible Meanings

- You want to expand your horizons at this time, perhaps travel, learn something new, or search for meaningful work. Act on this desire; do not wait around.
- A new partner arrives, either in business or love, who assists your progress.

Meanings When Reversed

Reversed, the globe falls out of your hand, suggesting little movement is being made to reach your goal. This may be because:

- You lack follow-through or persistence.
- Help hasn't come, or a partnership is not working out.
- Unexpected news arrives which causes delays or upsets to plans. Don't give up! Trust in your vision.

3 of Wands: Help Is On The Way

Key Meaning: The 3 of Wands indicates help is on the way. Perhaps you need someone's guidance, practical help, money, or connections. Good news; the cavalry is coming!

The Card: A man stands on a mountaintop, looking out to sea. When this card appears, it means you have enacted the plan you hatched in the 2 of Wands. There is progress because your ships are coming in. They are delivering fresh resources, providing you with the tools to expand further than you initially dared to dream. Excitement is building, and there is a scent of success in the air. There is no turning back now!

Karina Says: Momentum is building; you should be prepared for events to take off suddenly. Don't panic if things happen faster than you dared hope; all will turn out magically well.

Other Possible Meanings

- You start work in an area which involves foreign travel or overseas business dealings.
- You are inspired by an idea which unites all three elements of life – body, mind and spirit.

Meanings When Reversed

When reversed, the boats are less noticeable, and two of the wands drop away. We are back to square one – the single Ace of Wands.

- One step forward, two steps back. You experience delays or problems putting plans into action. This is not a green light to give up, but rather a sign to take time to reassess and regroup.
- Are you relying too much on hope and not enough on practical action?

4 of Wands: Cause For Celebration!

Key Meaning: The 4 of Wands indicates there is, or soon will be, cause for celebration.

The Card: What a happy scene! There is an air of festive celebration in this card, as we are greeted by the people waiting beyond the archway of wands and flowers. This card delivers good news; a reason to party with the people you love! You may be celebrating the completion of a work project, or something closer to home like an engagement, marriage, or graduation. Your home environment is happy at this time, and you can relax and enjoy the fruits of your labour.

Karina Says: Remember to be present when you spend time with friends and family. By that I mean, not distracted by other things. Give them your attention because today is the stuff of tomorrow's memories.

Other Possible Meanings

- You will be moving house or location. Sometimes, this card predicts a new holiday home.
- If you are going on vacation, everything turns out well.

Meanings When Reversed

Traditionally this card is so happy; it remains pretty much unaltered when reversed. Once the celebration is over, however, there may be a sense of *What now? Where do I go from here,* or *What do I focus on next?*

5 of Wands: Fight For What You Want

Key Meaning: The 5 of Wands indicates you need to be prepared to fight for what you want. All it takes is a little courage and staying power.

The Card: We see a group of men fighting in what appears to be a mock battle. Pumped with adrenaline, they are stimulated by a bit of healthy competition. When this card turns up, it says be prepared to battle for what you want. 5 is a dynamic and energetic number in Tarot and heralds unpredictable change. Your goals are achievable but may require a blend of persistence and flexibility. Sometimes, this card represents being caught off guard by a conflict, argument, or simply being unprepared for the difficulty of a situation.

Karina Says: When we look for slights, we tend to find them. If others are increasingly annoying you, perhaps it is time to look in the mirror for solutions. When we are quick to anger or feel defensive, it is usually a sign that we (ourselves) are uncertain or unhappy. Ask the Tarot for guidance; pick another card to help you navigate to a happier place.

Other Possible Meanings

- A disagreement with others arises.
- There are disruptions to your travel plans.

Meanings When Reversed

This is one of the few cards in Tarot where a reversal is better! Upside down, the men lay down their wands and harmony is restored.

- An argument, struggle, or period of stress comes to an end.
- You have won and can claim your prize.

6 of Wands: Victory

Key Meaning: The 6 of Wands indicates victory! Whatever you have been working towards – for example, a marriage proposal, promotion, or award – you receive your prize.

The Card: The 6 of Wands is one of the most exciting cards in the Tarot deck! The crowds gather to cheer, as a horseman rides into town, wearing a victory wreath on his head. He comes bearing good news, and announces that your dream is about to come true. Whether personal or work-related, whatever you have put effort into finally blossoms into something wonderful. Occasionally, it even means fame or wider public recognition in the world.

Karina Says: This is not a time for modesty or down-playing your abilities. Occasionally, it is good to allow your ego out to play. Delight in what you are achieving; recognise how well you are doing, and allow the feeling to propel you higher and further.

Other Possible Meanings

- Now is a good time to adopt a leadership role. You have what it takes!
- The outcome of a legal case is successful in your favour.
- If you take a journey out of town, it results in good news.

Meanings When Reversed

A reversal causes our victor to fall off his horse, and the parade is delayed until he can regain his saddle.

- News or plans are delayed; you must wait a little longer.
- Are you feeling too tired to pull off a victory? Rest and restore your balance.
- Are you resisting taking on a leadership role? Do not be too modest.

7 of Wands: Believe In Yourself

Key Meaning: The 7 of Wands encourages you to believe in yourself and to keep pushing ahead.

The Card: A man defends himself from multiple attackers, reflecting perhaps your sense that others do not have your back. This card reminds us that when we begin to succeed in life – whether personally or in business – it can provoke jealousy and competitiveness in others. You may be working or studying in a competitive area or doing well in another way. Notice that the man is in a superior position on top of the hill. This means that you are in a stronger place than you may think; so believe in what you are doing, and do not be distracted by petty minds around you. Do not be tempted to drop your standards just to make them more comfortable. Keep doing what you are doing.

Karina Says: The world does not need more of the same, it needs brave new thinkers, healers, and people who are passionate about progress. Will you remain safe in your existence – avoiding risk and the possible disapproval of others – or will you grab a wand and lead the way?

Other Possible Meanings

- This is the card you want to see if you are worried about your energy or motivation level. Yes, you have the stamina to keep going; don't give up now. You are far more capable than you realise.
- Stand your ground, and do not change your mind.

Meanings When Reversed

When reversed, the wand falls out of your hand, and your defence slips away.

- You feel able to let your defences down.
- You are comparing yourself to others and find yourself lacking. Rather than being depressed, can I recommend you be inspired!
- You walk away from a fight. This may be a good thing!
- You are working in an area or on a project which is less competitive.

8 of Wands: The Path Is Clear

Key Meaning: The 8 of Wands indicates the path is clear for your dreams to manifest.

The Card: We see 8 wands sailing through the sky over rolling hills and water. There are no obstacles in the way. This dynamic picture of motion predicts something wonderful coming, and soon. What is it that you been waiting for? Whatever it is – a job, business idea, personal project, or love life – it now takes off at great speed. Nothing stands between you and success. Prepare to be swept off your feet because this promises to be one heck of a ride!

Karina Says: You will realise soon that there is no longer anything in the way of you, and the life you dream of. Do not resist what comes to you now.

Other Possible Meanings

- If career is a priority, you can expect rapid advancement at this time.
- You take a trip, by plane, which expands your horizons. Even if you are not travelling, you may expand your mind in other ways.
- You are struck by cupid's love arrow. This is the beginning of a passionate love affair. Occasionally, this card means your lover comes from overseas.

Meanings When Reversed

Reversed, the arrows move in the wrong direction causing disruptions and delays.

- Your travel plans are delayed.
- Your energy is scattered; slow down and prioritise your goals more carefully.

9 of Wands: Keep Going

IX of Wands

Key Meaning: The 9 of Wands advises you to keep going. You are closer to realising your dream than you know.

The Card: A wounded man has fortified his rear with a row of wands. These wands represent past actions, implying he has had to fight to reach this point in life. The 9 of Wands says 'so far, so good'. You have battle wounds but you have become stronger and more special for it. A little extra push and you will achieve everything you want. The majority of your troubles are behind you now. Of course, you may still meet with a few obstacles, but they should be relatively minor in comparison.

Karina Says: You stand, now, hovering on the threshold between two worlds: the physical and spiritual. Whatever you do to improve your earthly life, at this time, will also draw you closer to the spiritual realm. This is the dawn of an awakening.

Other Possible Meanings

- This is the card you want to see when you are wondering: *How much more effort do I have to make?* The answer is, just a little more ...

- Trust in the basic goodness of people. Sure, some people can be unpleasant, but the majority are good at heart. Allow people into your life.

Meanings When Reversed

Upside down, the wands drop away, and your defences are down.

- Your physical defences are compromised; a weakened immune system makes you prone to illness and the flu. Take time out and rest.

- You feel at a dead end, and not sure what to do next. Pick another card for guidance.

10 of Wands: Feeling Exhausted

Key Meaning: The 10 of Wands indicates you feel exhausted and world-weary. The good news is, there is light at the end of the tunnel. You are on the home stretch to happier days.

The Card: An exhausted man makes his way home, bent down and head buried in the 10 of Wands he is carrying. When this card appears, it means you are shouldering a lot of responsibilities. It may be that you are happy to do so because you are ambitious to get ahead at work, or you want to look after your family's needs. Your heart is in the right place. Alternatively, you may be struggling under the strain and cannot see a way out. The good news is, you will not have to carry this load forever. Eventually, good things will emerge.

Karina Says: Are there others around you who could be doing more? Perhaps you worry they are not capable, or worse you fear not being needed? Either way, be prepared to release your burdens when the time is right. Sometimes, the noblest way to give, is to allow others to help themselves.

Other Possible Meanings

- Your enthusiasm is dying under the weight of duty or work.
- You do not see the woods for the trees. Take time out to consider the bigger picture.

Meanings When Reversed

The 10 of Wands, when reversed, delivers good news! You drop your wands and are freed from the burdens associated with them.

- Life eases, and you are released of certain burdens.
- You let go of the guilt and the feeling that you have to do it all.
- Alternatively, are you denying how much you do? Burying your head in the sand?

Page of Wands: Exciting News

Page of Wands

Key Meaning: The Page of Wands delivers exciting news of a new endeavour. This is particularly welcome if you have been feeling bored or lacking in direction.

The Card: The Page holds his wand, contemplating the information he is about to deliver to you. This card often signals the beginning of passion; perhaps you become captivated by a new hobby, project, or person. It can also indicate news of a more daily kind, such as the confirmation of an appointment you have been waiting for, or travel arrangements coming through. Occasionally, this enthusiastic messenger delivers news which is completely out of the blue.

Personality: When the Page refers to a person, he or she is young, enthusiastic, impulsive, and easily bored. They are at their best when they follow their passion, particularly when it comes to career. However, it may take some time before they finally settle on their true calling. Wands are associated with the fire sign in astrology, so this may represent an Aries, Leo, or Sagittarius.

Karina Says: A life without passion is not living. It is merely existing.

Other Possible Meanings

- You got the job!
- You passed your exams.

Meanings When Reversed

When the Page is reversed, it means we are resisting the news he delivers.

- You are finding reasons not to make the effort to change, despite change being what you crave. Draw another card for guidance on how to overcome this block.
- Very occasionally, it signals someone is gossiping about you. Or, are you the gossip?

Knight of Wands: Sudden Movement

Key Meaning: The Knight of Wands indicates sudden movement, usually after a period of inactivity or delays.

The Card: This brave Knight surges on his horse, wand raised and ready for action. When this card appears, a new adventure is approaching, and the Knight warns you to be ready. The change he promises will be exciting, but may require courage as your daily routines are disrupted. If you have been stuck in limbo for a while, then this Knight is a breath of fresh air, heralding the end of stagnation. Notice the three pyramids in the background; they represent the power of body, mind, and spirit. Wherever this journey leads, it is sure to leave you feeling satisfied on many levels.

Personality: When the Knight of Wands refers to a person, he is a young man (30 or under) who is generous and does everything in a big way. He is hot-headed, creative, and has oodles of energy. As a lover, he can be flirty and hard to tie down, but because he is so much fun we tend to forgive him. The Knight's tunic is decorated with salamanders; symbolic of fire and passion. Wands are associated with fire signs in astrology, so he may represent a Sagittarius, Aries, or Leo.

Karina Says: If you move ahead now, fear and doubt will transform into courage and confidence.

Other Possible Meanings

- You have been craving excitement, and now it comes! What happens next could, in fact, be life changing, even if you don't yet see how.
- Honour your thirst for adventure and your need to break free.
- You change residence; for some it means emigration.

Meanings When Reversed

Reversed, the poor horsey falls on his back, the wand falls out of the Knight's hand, and the pyramids point downward. Power and energy are lost.

- You lack the motivation to accept what is on offer. Draw another card for guidance.
- You feel overwhelmed by all the comings and goings. Take it one day at a time.
- A journey, action, or change of residence is delayed.

Queen of Wands: You Feel Optimistic

Queen of Wands

Key Meaning: The Queen of Wands indicates you feel optimistic about life and confident that you can achieve whatever you want. This positive can-do attitude is not misplaced, you are right to trust the feeling.

The Card: The Queen sits on her throne, holding the Ace of Wands in one hand and a sunflower in the other. The wand tells us she has grabbed whatever opportunities have presented themselves and the sunflower indicates her life is blooming as a result. Notice the black cat, observing those approaching the throne. The cat represents intuition and advises you not to neglect *your* intuition when dealing with others. It does not matter if you are a homemaker or CEO; embrace your natural sixth sense. When the Queen appears, it means you are in a powerful position to attract whatever you desire, in any area of your life – business, home, relationships, personal development, and spiritual growth.

Personality: A warm and loving woman, although at times she can be bossy and tends to over-manage children, partners, and friends. She is friendly, but not overly so. She is attractive and can charm the pants off anyone when it is to her advantage. This Queen has a vibrant spirit and can rise to the top of her career or community. Her fiery nature makes her a passionate friend but a fearsome enemy! In astrology, wands are associated with fire signs, so she may represent a Leo, Sagittarius, or Aries.

Karina Says: If you do not resonate with the card – know that the qualities of this Queen lie within you; waiting to emerge if you embrace them.

Other Possible Meanings

- Any business idea or project you turn your hand to, now, will be successful.
- You are demanding more of the world and are less prepared to put up with second-best.
- Now is a good time to invest in yourself, by embarking on some personal programme of study.

Meanings When Reversed

Reversed, this Queen is still powerful but a little less organised and confident. Be cool, and trust your judgement. You do not need to do everything at once.

King of Wands: You Feel Ambitious

Key Meaning: The King of Wands indicates the spark of ambition has ignited within you. This masculine energy makes you feel powerful and motivated.

The Card: The King sits on his throne holding the Ace of Wands, a reminder perhaps of how far he has come. His cloak is richly decorated with lions and salamanders, symbols of power and courage. When the King of Wands appears, it means your confidence is soaring, and you are finding ways to express the real you. Where the Queen tends to represent fulfilment on a more personal level, the King predicts wider recognition from the community and world at large. This is a good time to focus your attention on projects which give you an opportunity to promote your ideas (eventually) to a wider audience.

Personality: A mature man who is well-travelled, confident, and enthusiastic. He makes a wonderful mentor and is good at inspiring others. Wands are connected to astrology's fire signs, so he may represent an Aries, Leo, or Sagittarius. He has a forceful presence, the sort of person you notice when he enters a room. Famous fire signs include Barack Obama, Bill Clinton and Robert De Niro. The King is a good communicator which is why he does well in sales, marketing, and self-employment.

Karina Says: Eventually, there comes a time when we instinctively *know*, it is now or never. That we must act or find another dream. Now is *that* time.

Other Possible Meanings

- If you are involved in business negotiations, they turn out well.
- Express your ideas and create something which is very different to what already exists.
- This is a good time to lead group activities.

Meanings When Reversed

Reversed, everything falls away, and our King becomes pessimistic and loses enthusiasm.

- You feel the loss of identity, due perhaps to retirement, unemployment, or business woes.
- Is ego or vanity standing in your way of learning and progressing?

As all court cards are minor cards, it means you can turn the situation around with a better mindset. Draw another card for guidance on how to correct this imbalance.

CUPS

Ace of Cups: New Passion

Key Meaning: The Ace of Cups signifies a new passion is about to enter your life.

The Card: The miraculous hand of an unseen Power appears out of the cloud and offers you a cup. You are being invited to drink from this overflowing cup of abundance. Jets of water flow from the chalice into a larger sea of water. Water represents our emotions and deepest desires, and your water – it seems – runs deep and plentiful. A white dove, a symbol of the Holy Spirit, bestows a blessing from above in the form of a wafer. When the Ace of Cups appears, you are advised to open your heart and embrace whatever happens now. This could be the romance of a lifetime, the renewal of an existing relationship, or the birth of a child. Or it may be a work or study opportunity which impassions you. The Ace of Cups often appears when we are feeling lost or vaguely dissatisfied with life. Do not worry, the Holy Spirit says, I know exactly what you need. Trust that this is the beginning of a life-altering journey.

Karina Says: What you seek is the holy grail of happiness: more love and a fulfilling purpose. Fortunately, these worthy objectives are within your reach now. Remember, money and material security are merely the by-products of living a life with passion.

Other Possible Meanings

- A new passion is about to enter your life – love, career, or interest.
- If you are attracted to spiritual matters at this time, it is because you are going through an awakening.
- If you have had an inspirational idea for a new business, project, or book... go for it!

Meanings When Reversed

When the Ace of Cups is reversed, the water spills out and your enthusiasm along with it!

- If you are in a relationship, your love has eroded over time. The relationship needs attention if it is to recover.
- If you are single, love is on the way, but not just yet! Be patient.
- If you started a new relationship, this romance will take some time to develop – go with the flow and enjoy the trip.
- If you are interested in spirituality, your psychic abilities are blocked at this time. Draw another card for guidance on what to do.

2 of Cups: Your Relationship Blossoms

II of Cups

Key Meaning: The 2 of Cups signifies the blossoming of a romance or business relationship.

The Card: A couple moves closer, and raise their glasses to toast one another. A winged lion's head, representing earthly and spiritual love, presides over the toast. This is the union of two souls who are different and, yet, complement each other. Whatever the Ace of Cups delivered in the past, has moved forward now and events really begin to take off. Your romance deepens as a commitment is made. Perhaps you move in together, get engaged, or marry. In business, a working relationship turns out well and leads to mutual prosperity. Occasionally, this card appears when you have been going through a period of self-healing. You have conquered inner demons and what remains is self-love and acceptance in all its glory.

Karina Says: When the flower blossoms, the bees will come. This is the summer of your life; a beautiful and harmonious time.

Other Possible Meanings

- If you asked how someone feels about you, they feel the same way you do.
- If you had an argument with someone recently, don't worry, you will make up.

Meanings When Reversed

When reversed, the couple still want to connect, but the water is flowing out of the cups. This signifies the relationship is losing momentum. There may be disagreements or misunderstandings. However, as the 2 of Cups is not a destiny card, you can (with a little effort) reverse this decline. If you need guidance on *how*, then draw another card.

3 of Cups: Cause For Celebration

Key Meaning: The 3 of Cups signifies there is cause for celebration!

The Card: Three maidens dance and hold their cups high in a toast to friendship and the good life. At their feet lie an abundance of fruits and garlands; the fruits of their labour. When the 3 of Cups appears, it means that there is cause for celebration. Perhaps you receive good news; the reward for some effort you have made. Or maybe you are attending a wedding, party, or a night out with friends. Either way, loosen up and enjoy it! On a larger scale, this is a good time to embrace the lighter, brighter, social side of life. If you are single, you can meet someone at a social event or night out. In work, it pays to network. Resist falling into the trap of thinking that socialising is a waste of time. Your sparkle meter is revving, so go out and dazzle people.

Karina Says: When it feels that life is getting on top of you, go sit in some pretty place in nature. Remind yourself that you are one of the lucky souls chosen to have an experience on the most beautiful planet in the Universe. When we love life, it tends to love us back.

Other Possible Meanings

- You receive news which is cause for celebration.
- You reconnect with old friends or family, and it cheers you up.

Meanings When Reversed

Reversed, our fair maidens are partied-out and exhausted.

- You have over-indulged, and it is time to get back to a healthier routine.
- You need to recharge your batteries; take time out and reconnect with friends.

4 of Cups: Waiting For Change

Key Meaning: The 4 of Cups signifies you feel bored and are waiting for something or someone to spark change in your life.

The Card: A man sits under a tree with his arms and legs folded, looking bored and dissatisfied. Three cups stand before him, and a fourth one is magically proffered out of the blue. Yet, he seems unimpressed by this amazing opportunity, or perhaps he is so lost in thought he does not notice it. When the 4 of Cups appears, it means the cups from which you have been symbolically drinking have run dry. What once made you happy no longer does so. The issue is, you are not sure what to do or where to begin to find happiness on a deeper level. You are like Buddha, meditating under a tree waiting for enlightenment. The 4 of Cups advises you to pay more attention to what is going on around you because a new opportunity is near and there is a chance you could miss it. In particular, new social contacts are open to you, and if you make the effort to connect, it will take you in an unexpected new direction. These people are your doorway to a new and exciting chapter in your life, even if it does seem unlikely at first.

Karina Says: Most of us want change; it is just the effort required to make those changes that we tend to resist. Change is hard and sometimes painful, and yet it is the only way to transform the dreary into something magical.

Other Possible Meanings

- Be careful not to miss the opportunity under your nose due to lack of motivation.
- Any time you spend now on self-development will not be wasted.

Meanings When Reversed

Reversed, the man falls on his feet and is spurred into action. This signifies you emerge from your rut and head in a new direction. You are motivated now to chase new goals and friendships.

5 of Cups: Feeling Sad

Key Meaning: The 5 of Cups indicates you feel sad or disappointed. The sun will rise again.

The Card: A man in a dark cloak stares dejectedly down at three cups before him which have spilled over. He appears so sad, as he focuses on the fallen cups, that he does not notice the two upright cups behind him – possible future sources of happiness. When the 5 of Cups appears, it means you have suffered a loss or disappointment of some kind. Maybe someone has let you down, or your dream has not worked out as you hoped; a friendship or relationship has broken up, or you have suffered a bereavement. Allow your tears to flow and give vent to your emotions. The sooner you do, the sooner you can heal and take advantage of those upright cups behind you. Even if the present seems bleak, you will have things to look forward to. When the 5 of Cups appears, it may be worth asking: *Can this situation be saved or should I move on?* Draw another card for guidance if you are not sure.

Karina Says: Suffering *anywhere* is the concern of humans *everywhere*. Raise your eyes from your concerns and cast them towards the suffering of others. In the pursuit of helping others, you resolve your own problems.

Other Possible Meanings

- If someone has let you down, know that they were not trying to hurt you on purpose. However, this does not mean they will be trustworthy in the future.

Meanings When Reversed

When the 5 of Cups is reversed, everything is much better. It heralds the return of optimism and happy days.

- You are filled with hope and energy. Now, you can get on with your life.
- Rifts with others are healed; let bygones be bygones.
- You make new friends who open your eyes to new experiences.

6 of Cups: Blast From The Past

Key Meaning: The 6 of Cups signifies a blast from the past. Either you meet someone from the past or an opportunity presents itself which has a connection to your past.

The Card: A little boy hands a cup of flowers to a little girl. Nearby, five other cups, filled with flowers, signify he is bearing gifts of the heart. The old-fashioned village triggers feelings of childhood and nostalgia for the olden days. When the 6 of Cups appears, you are likely to meet someone from your past; this could be a friend, an ex-lover, or a reunion with family. This is a happy occasion and raises sweet memories. Alternatively, if you are presented with an opportunity now (for example, a new relationship, change of location, or job), it is likely to have some connection to your past. Any relationship you begin now is a soulmate connection, and it feels like you have known each other before. If not in this life, then in a past life. This card often turns up to confirm a past life connection to a place or person.

Karina Says: Live life and do not get hung up on age. Your soul is timeless, and any age is the right age to start doing what you want to do.

Other Possible Meanings

- If you are confused about work, the advice is to go back to your original training or plans.
- If you are thinking about moving back to where you grew up, go for it!

Meanings When Reversed

When reversed, the past is turned upside down. This can be a good thing!

- Old hurts and wounds are released, and you can finally move on.
- You are growing up, depending less on family for support and guidance.

7 of Cups: Make A Choice!

Key Meaning: The 7 of Cups signifies you need to make a choice in order to move forward with the next phase of your life.

The Card: Seven cups appear to you out of the clouds. Seven tempting options and you are asked to choose one. Should you focus on the snake (symbol of desire and temptation), the castle (family), jewels (money), dragon (meditation and spiritual path), victory wreath (success and fame), the woman (love), or the hidden figure (adventure)? When the 7 of Cups appears, it indicates you feel confused and uncertain about life. The danger here is that you are overwhelmed by too many choices and, as a result, end up doing nothing (and come away empty handed). While there may be no obvious choice or clear direction at this time, whichever path you choose has the potential to excite you. This is because all paths lead to Rome; they simply offer different routes and scenery. The key is to make a choice; choose any path and get on with it. If you struggle to choose, pick another card for guidance.

Karina Says: In life, there are rarely *right* or *wrong* decisions. It is the effort we put in, once we have made a decision, that makes the difference.

Other Possible Meanings

- Your imagination is working overtime. This is a good time to put creative projects into action.
- Time to ignore distractions and focus on what you need to do.

Meanings When Reversed

Reversed, the dark figure in the card suddenly appears more dominant. This signifies you have taken control and made a decision. Now you can finally move forward. When the 7 of Cups is reversed it always means you have made the right decision, so do not second-guess yourself. If things do not go as smoothly as you hope, do not give up.

8 of Cups: Walk Away

Key Meaning: The 8 of Cups reflects your desire to walk away from a situation in search of something more meaningful.

The Card: A man walks, stick in hand, towards the mountains. Eight cups are neatly stacked behind him, representing all that was once dear to him. He is not leaving out of fear or necessity, but rather because he senses there is more to experience beyond the mountain. When the 8 of Cups turns up, it means you crave more passion, stimulation, adventure, and love in your life. This card often appears when someone is going through a spiritual awakening. Notice the lunar eclipse above the mountains which casts a strange light and heightens the emotional experience. You could end up abandoning your routine, job, relationships – even your belief system – all in search of something more spiritually fulfilling. You have no way of knowing at this time what lies beyond the mountain, so a leap of faith is required. One thing you can be sure of, is that this promises to be a great adventure.

Karina Says: Do you sometimes doubt your ability to hear your spirit guides? If so, remember you *are* a spirit, wrapped in a human body. So, of course, you can communicate with other spirits. In fact, when you think about it, it is as natural as walking and talking.

Other Possible Meanings

- This is a good time go on vacation or a retreat and recharge your batteries.
- If you are drawn to spiritual work, heed the calling.
- If you are moving location, this is the start of a new era.

Meanings When Reversed

When the 8 of Cups is reversed, the man returns from the mountains and reconnects with the people and place he left behind. The spiritual awakening is complete; you flip back and reconnect with the world. Whatever you have learnt on your journey, you can now apply in a practical way with great success.

9 of Cups: Your Wish Comes True

Key Meaning: The 9 of Cups is the luckiest card in Tarot. Yes, your wish comes true!

The Card: A well-fed man sits contentedly, surrounded by his cups. The 9 of Cups is everyone's favourite card in Tarot because it means your wish is granted. What did you ask for? More money, a job, a new relationship, better health, or just happiness? Well, good fortune is on your side because you are about to receive what you truly seek. When this card appears, it reflects a general increase in success and luck in your life. People start to see you as someone who has 'made it' in your own area of expertise, and they sit up and take notice. You have great potential at this time to inspire people with what you have learnt. Your role is not just to enjoy yourself, but to capitalise on your abilities and good fortune and spread your light.

Karina Says: The Universe sends this Irish blessing to you today: *May good luck be your friend in whatever you do, and may trouble always be a stranger to you.*

Other Possible Meanings

- Luck is on your side; make the most of it.
- If you are over-indulging on food or drink, cut back a little.
- You have come a long way, but do not become complacent. There is still much for you to achieve.

Meanings When Reversed

When the 9 of Cups is reversed, your wish is delayed or does not happen in the way you expect. A little patience is necessary; the Universe needs more time to manifest what you truly want. For example, you may not get the job you hope for, but an even better option turns up later.

10 of Cups: Happy Ever After

Key Meaning: The 10 of Cups signifies you are on the path to achieving your happy ever after.

The Card: A man and woman embrace as their two children play nearby. There is a great sense of joy in this card as the family give thanks – under a rainbow filled with cups – for the good things in their lives. When this card appears, it means you are on the right path to achieving lasting happiness and success, both emotionally and materially. Whatever situation you asked about – a home you love, babies, marriage, family, health or fulfilling work – the 10 of Cups always represents a positive outcome. Yes, you will have what your heart desires. There is expansion in every area of your life; a magic rainbow is sprinkling miracles all around.

Karina Says: Powerful angels have chosen to protect you and those you love. Of course, no life is 'perfect', but you will experience more blessings and opportunities than most at this time.

Other Possible Meanings

- A new or current romance leads to marriage.
- Your children do well at school and find happiness in the world.
- If you asked, *Will I have children?* The answer is Yes.
- A business idea or career change is worth pursuing. You will be successful and enjoy it.
- A family gathering or arrival of visitors goes well.

Meanings When Reversed

When the 10 of Cups is reversed, there are delays to achieving your happy ever after scenario.

- For example, a house move does not go through, wedding proposals are delayed, there are squabbles within the family, or a financial problem arises. Draw another card for guidance on how to deal with the situation.
- Feeling sad (empty nest syndrome) as a child leaves home.

Page of Cups: News Of Love

Page of Cups

Key Meaning: The Page of Cups signifies news of a kind which makes you feel loved and appreciated.

The Card: This light-hearted Page smiles as he listens to whatever news the fish is imparting. The calm water and clear sky suggest the sort of news that makes you feel good about yourself. Someone may make their affections for you clear. Either they ask you out on a date or declare their love after a few dates. If you are in a long-term relationship, this could be a proposal or a surprise pregnancy! Love is all around! When the Page of Cups appears and you just had a job interview – good news – they loved you! You got the job. Now you have a growing sense of optimism and belief that life will turn out exactly as you want it to. This optimism is reflected back to you, as you attract more and more happy events. The Page of Cups also guides you to make the effort to meet new people at this time, either socially or in connection with your work. New contacts will expand your life and encourage you to do things you would not normally do.

Personality: When the Page refers to a person, he or she is young, sensitive, and highly psychic. They are creative day-dreamers prone to getting lost in their own world. Then again, they could also be the next Mozart or JK Rowling! This young person is easy-going, and children and animals are drawn to them like magnets. Cups are associated with water signs in astrology, so this may represent a Pisces, Scorpio, or Cancer.

Karina Says: Intuition is your shortcut to success. Trust your gut feelings, in love, life, and work.

Other Possible Meanings

- News arrives of a pregnancy, or the birth of a child within the family.
- Your psychic and mediumship abilities are unfolding. You are receiving messages from the other side.

Meanings When Reversed

When the Page of Cups is reversed, the fish falls out of the cup, so we do not get to hear what he has to say. This means news is delayed.

Knight of Cups: Your Love Life Improves

Knight of Cups

Key Meaning: The Knight of Cups signifies your love life is about to improve.

The Card: A handsome Knight rides across the countryside on his gallant horse. He holds out a cup, a symbol of emotional devotion. Whenever a Knight appears in Tarot, regardless of suit, it heralds movement after a period of stagnation. As this fair Knight is the keeper of hearts, it means your love life is being resuscitated! Depending on your circumstances, this could mean a new romance after a period of singledom. If there is no love interest on your radar at the moment, then buckle up as he or she is heading your way. However, if you do fancy someone – now is the time to strike! Don't wait around – let them know! If you are in a relationship, then expect a shakeup to your routines. This Knight says life is dull without an adventure or two; so, whatever excitement happens now, it will spice up your relationship and draw you closer.

Personality: When the Knight refers to a person, he is a young man (under 30) who is sensitive and a good communicator. He has a great sense of humour, is imaginative and creative. He could work in sales, or as a therapist, healer, artist or writer. He is a bit of a romantic dreamer, blessed with lots of ideas but can struggle to put them into action. Ideally, his partner should be more grounded and practical. Cups are associated with water signs in astrology, so this may represent a Pisces, Scorpio or Cancer.

Karina Says: Once in a lifetime, you meet someone who changes everything.

Other Possible Meanings

- If you asked: *Is this the person I will marry?* The answer is yes.
- If you asked: *Is my creation or idea ready to share with others?* The answer is yes.

Meanings When Reversed

Upside down, the Knight falls off his horse and loses his cool!

- When the Knight of Cups is reversed, and you asked about a particular person, then be careful. This guy is immature, unreliable, and fears commitment.
- If you asked about yourself, then it could be you who is blocking a healthy relationship. Perhaps you fear being hurt; or are you acting a little immaturely? Pick another card for guidance on what to do.

Queen of Cups: Trust Your Intuition

Queen of Cups

Key Meaning: The Queen of Cups signifies that your intuition is at an all-time high.

The Card: The Queen of Cups sits on her ornate throne, gazing into a beautiful cup. Notice how the cup is closed, signifying that her thoughts are in the realm of the unseen and unconscious world. She sits by the ocean, resting her feet on stones. This card has a dream-like quality; we are not sure if the Queen has dreamt this scene or if it is real. When the Queen of Cups appears, it means you are in the middle of a major spiritual transformation. Manifestation powers are at an all-time high, so be clear about what you want. If you can see it in your mind, you can hold it in your hand. Additionally, expect to receive intuitive messages in new ways, through touch, sight, hearing, and smell.

Personality: When the Queen refers to a person, she is kind and empathetic. She is a listener and carer, which is why she is considered the ideal wife and mother. Typically, she may work as a nurse, carer, therapist, counsellor, writer, or in fashion, as an interior designer, or stay-at-home mum. In astrology, cups are associated with water, so this may represent a Cancer, Scorpio or Pisces.

Karina Says: We are all connected by a silver cord to a greater power in the Universe. Think of this cord like a telephone line, through which we receive ideas and inspiration. Intuitive people receive more information because they have a better telephone connection.

Other Possible Meanings

- You have a psychic connection with someone overseas. This is why you think about each other at the same time.
- If you want to move house, your ideal home will be found closer to the sea, a lake, or river.

Meanings When Reversed

When the Queen of Cups is reversed, the waters are rough, and the tide is coming in too fast. It could be that you are emotionally out of whack and need to meditate or rest.

- You are stressing and worrying about things over which you have no control.
- Try not to over-react about the little things. Allow life to flow more easily.

King of Cups: Rise Up!

King of Cups

Key Meaning: The King of Cups announces: rise up and serve humanity!

The Card: The King sits on his throne, managing to keep afloat and serene despite the rough waters. A fish jumps out of the sea to peep at us, and a ship sails by in the background. Water represents emotions and deep feelings. When the King of Cups appears, it means you have the ability to navigate others through the choppy emotional waters of life. You may be doing this already, offering support and encouragement to family and friends. Or maybe it is the element of your job or voluntary work that you most enjoy. Know that higher powers have taken a special interest in you, and they are encouraging you to embrace this side of yourself. They ask you to leave the world a little better than you found it. If you are considering a new business, job, study, hobby or community project – ask, *how* will this help others? You may, for example, be drawn to counselling, healing, teaching, social work, writing, public speaking, or sales. Trust in your visions, and you will be spectacularly successful.

Personality: When the King refers to a person, he is a man over 30, who is kind and empathetic. Emotionally mature, he is sophisticated and interested in the arts. When this King turns up as a love interest, the relationship should be happy and successful. This is a soulmate connection. If the King is reversed as a love interest, he is not reliable, so be careful about becoming too involved. Cups are connected to astrology's water signs, so this may represent a Scorpio, Pisces or Cancer.

Karina Says: "I am endeavouring to see God through service of humanity; for I know that God is neither in heaven, nor down below, but in everyone." Mahatma Gandhi.

Meanings When Reversed

Reversed, the King of Cups is tossed into the sea and loses his emotional balance. This means you need to prioritise your own needs at this time. Try not to feel guilty about saying no to people; your energy is depleted, and you cannot continue to give without refuelling. Be gentle with yourself; take whatever time you need to recover. You will have plenty of time to save the world later!

SWORDS

Ace of Swords: Brilliant Ideas

Key Meaning: You are about to have a brilliant idea, or perhaps you have just had it! Either way, the Ace of Swords promises spectacular success as long as you follow through.

The Card: A hand appears out of the clouds offering you a sword. The sword is encircled with olive leaves and a crown; the symbols of victory. This card says, now is the time to embrace your power and commit to a cause, project, or new direction. Along the way, you will have many more moments of inspiration, and you will find the willpower to act on those too. This is an exciting new phase; so grab that sword, and claim your victory! The Ace of Swords also appears when you are struggling with an existing situation and are worried about your ability to cope. The answer is – YES YOU CAN!

Karina Says: The Gods do not take away problems, but they do give strength to those they wish to succeed. You are one of the chosen people. Take the sword and embrace your destiny.

Other Possible Meanings

- Swords rule communication. An opportunity appears to communicate your thoughts to others. This could be in your personal relationships, or a public speaking opportunity, published article, or book deal.
- As swords cut like knives, they are linked to surgery. If you are having an operation, rest assured all will turn out well.
- The crown on the tip of the sword looks like an engagement ring. Expect a wedding proposal soon!

Meanings When Reversed

Reversed, the crown slips off the sword indicating victory could take longer than expected.

- Be patient and do not push for an outcome. Allow the situation to unfold naturally.
- You feel confused and struggle to see a way forward. If you are a writer, this indicates writer's block. Pick another card for guidance on how to break this impasse.

2 of Swords: Face The Problem

Key Meaning: The 2 of Swords asks: *What issue are you avoiding?* Whatever it is, face it down! Whether you realise it, or not, worry has been sapping your energy and robbing your joy.

The Card: A blindfolded woman sits on a bench holding 2 swords. The blindfold prevents her from seeing what is in front of her. We have the feeling, however, that she does not want to see; if she did, she could simply remove the blindfold. The swords are held in a defensive manner suggesting she does not want to talk about the problem, and may even deny there is one. She sits alone in the dark with her back to the water. The water and moon represent emotions and intuition, so she is aware – at a deeper level – that something must be dealt with. The 2 of Swords guides you to address what is holding you back, no matter how painful or difficult this may be. Open your eyes, and your heart, and allow the light to shine on the issue – generally, when this card appears, the solution is right under your nose!

Karina Says: The worst decision is no decision. Just 'going along with things' is not a solution. It does not inspire you to improve the situation, nor does it motivate you to find something better. Indecision robs you of happiness and a sense of achievement. Do not fear making a wrong decision. Be very afraid however of making no decision.

Other Possible Meanings

- What are you putting off doing? Start now.
- You are involved in negotiations, but discussions come to a standstill.
- You are trying to keep out of other people's arguments. Chances are, you will still be called to broker the peace.

Meanings When Reversed

The 2 of Swords reversed is a lovely card! It means a decision has been taken and progress can finally be made!

- There is clarity now, and you can move forward.
- You are free to do what you want now.

3 of Swords: You Feel Sad

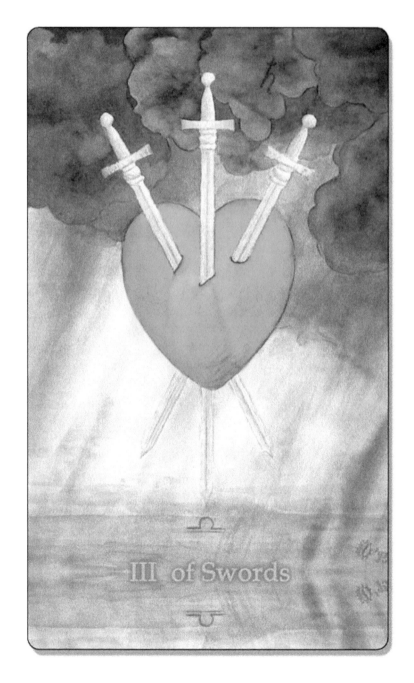

Key Meaning: The 3 of Swords represents sadness and disappointment. Something does not turn out as you hope. Allow the tears to flow so the healing can begin.

The Card: We see a heart pierced by three swords. The heart is a universal symbol of love, and when it is cut, there is a release of emotions – hurt, pain, grief, and a sense of loss. Heavy rain is falling, implying that tears need to be shed. Your suffering may be the result of a life-altering event, such as the loss of a loved one, or a relationship breakup. Or it could reflect a less dramatic and more immediate situation such as someone hurting your feelings, or disappointment at not getting the job or promotion you want. Either way, acknowledge your feelings so that the recovery can begin. If you are not sure what the source of your sorrow is, draw another card for guidance.

Karina Says: Sometimes sadness lingers and feels like it will never go away. And yet, when you look back in time, you will realise you have moved on.

Other Possible Meanings

- This card can herald the end of a marriage/serious relationship, but it can also indicate the physical separation of an otherwise happy couple due to other issues – like travel, or living in different locations.
- A child has moved away, and you are experiencing empty nest syndrome.
- Someone has hurt you, and you know there is no going back from here.
- You miss a loved one who has passed over. Grief counselling or a kind ear may help.

Meanings When Reversed

The 3 of Swords reversed is a much happier card and says you are moving past your difficulty. Your tender heart is in recovery.

4 of Swords: Time to Rest

Key Meaning: The 4 of Swords advises you to rest. Take time out to re-charge your body, mind, and spirit.

The Card: A knight lies eerily still on a tomb; his eyes closed and his hands raised in the prayer position. Some people are frightened by this card because they think it predicts death. It does not! The knight is very much alive and is simply recuperating from a battle. The 4 of Swords says you should rest now, even retreat from the world. Silence is golden. Perhaps you have been busy, stressed out, or are recovering from illness or surgery. This is a good time to slow your pace and ponder the future. Notice that the knight seems very much at peace, reflecting on what has gone before. He encourages you to unwind and leave the tension behind you. There is no point in fighting yesterday's battles. See this as a period of relaxation, recovery, and expansion, in preparation for a new adventure.

Karina Says: Prayer is when you talk to God and meditation is when He talks to you. Listen in silence and be open to the guidance you receive.

Other Possible Meanings

- Your planned holiday or spiritual retreat is very restful.
- If you are a writer or social influencer, pay attention to your dreams because you are downloading ideas from the Universe which need to be passed on.
- You are bored by the things you once enjoyed. This is a sign that you are evolving and changing. Do not feel guilty about letting go and starting afresh.

Meanings When Reversed

The knight falls off the tomb, and springs into action. He says: 'I'm back!'

- The end of recovery or isolation. You re-enter the world.
- Sleepless nights, disturbing dreams, or insomnia. Draw another card for the source of this disturbance.
- When reversed, the knight is now floating, indicating an out-of-body experience. Perhaps this is something that interests you?

5 of Swords: Feeling Angry

* Warning: Meant with Love *

Key Meaning: The 5 of Swords signifies you feel frustrated and this is leading to angry outbursts.

The Card: What a bleak picture this card presents! A warrior watches as two opponents walk dejectedly away. The sky is stormy and the wind is howling, indicating that some violent outburst has just taken place. The 5 of Swords is not the easiest card to receive, because it requires some soul-searching at a time when you may not be in the frame of mind to listen! You are guided to ask yourself honestly: *What is the real underlying cause of my frustration?* Resist the temptation to blame others (including me for writing this message!). When we are unhappy with ourselves, we tend to lash out at other people or allow jealousy to blinker us. This card typically reflects conflict, disconnection, and a breakdown of communication. When the 5 of Swords appears, it cautions you to be careful with your words because you may not be able to take them back. The good news is, you have the power to transform this situation for the better. Draw another card for guidance on how best to achieve this.

Karina Says: We are all hitch-hikers through time and space. We come together for different reasons and part when our paths move in different directions. Some relationships are destined to change, and we must accept these transitions gracefully and without accusation.

Other Possible Meanings

- Other people are increasingly 'getting on your nerves'. At least consider the possibility that the real issue is you.
- Be careful not to hurt people with your words. One day they may not forgive you.
- A friendship or relationship parts with bitter words.

Meanings When Reversed

The 5 of Swords is one of the few cards in Tarot where the meaning is not changed by a reversal. If anything, it can suggest that you are denying your role in the conflicts around you.

6 of Swords: Better Times Are Coming

Key Meaning: The 6 of Swords signifies better times are coming as you row into peaceful waters.

The Card: A ferryman rows a woman and her child across water. The water on the right of the boat is choppy, but notice the sea ahead is much calmer. This tells us that the passengers are moving away from difficulties, crossing from one land to another. When this card appears, it means you are transitioning from one place to another. This could literally mean moving location, or – as the swords represent our mindset – it could mean you are moving on emotionally and viewing life differently. At this time, it is not possible to predict what lies ahead because your view is obscured by the swords stacked on the boat. Yet, whatever turns up, it promises to be much brighter than what you are leaving behind.

Karina Says: A smooth sea never made a skilful sailor. Even if you feel shaken by events, know that you are stronger for it. The Universe has some pretty exciting plans in store for you, you just need to be ready to capitalise on them.

Other Possible Meanings

- You have a happy vacation or trip overseas. In some cases, this card predicts emigration.
- Expect visitors to arrive from overseas.
- You are moving past an unpleasant situation, job, health problem, or family issue.

Meanings When Reversed

When the 6 of Swords is reversed, the boat sinks! You are not yet able to row into better days.

- No change yet. Your dreams or plans are postponed. Wait for better timing.
- You feel stuck in a rut and do not know how to move forward. Draw another card for guidance.

7 of Swords: Someone Is Being Sneaky

Key Meaning: The 7 of Swords signifies that someone close to you is being sneaky and not telling you the truth.

The Card: What you see is what you get with this card! A thief tip-toes away with a bunch of swords he has stolen from an encampment. He leaves behind a couple of swords, evidence of his foul play. When this card appears, it indicates that someone is lying or not telling you the whole truth. Chances are, your intuition will have picked up on this, even if you tried to dismiss it.

Karina Says: Sometimes we avoid seeking the truth because we do not want to destroy our illusions. No matter how difficult the truth may be, it always leaves you more empowered in the end.

Other Possible Meanings

- You, or someone close to you, is having a secret love affair.
- Someone is talking about you behind your back.

If you do not resonate with any of the above meanings, then the 7 of Swords is trying to guide you to be more cautious in another area (for example finances, property, or business). Draw an additional card for more information.

Meanings When Reversed

When reversed, the swords drop out of the thief's arms and land back with their rightful owners.

- Dishonesty comes to light; truth is revealed. Now at least everyone can move forward.
- You receive an apology.
- Stolen goods are returned to you.

8 of Swords: Fear Is Holding You Back

Key Meaning: The 8 of Swords signifies that fear is holding you back from embracing your sparkling destiny. Release the fear and trust the Universe will support you.

The Card: A woman stands on marshy ground. She is blindfolded, and her arms are tied behind her back. In the distance, there is a pretty castle – an Aladdin's cave filled with exciting possibilities. But before she can explore it, she must free herself of her binds. Notice, in the picture, that she is not encircled completely by swords, there is an opening in front of her. This leads us to feel that she could save herself if only she would do something about it. We are reminded, by this card, that fear can paralyse us and render us helpless. When the 8 of Swords turns up, it says you feel caged in, but are too scared to make the necessary changes to escape your situation. It may be a case of the devil you know is better than the devil you don't? Fear of the unknown can feel like a bigger threat than the hardship you are currently enduring. The good news is, when the 8 of Swords appears, it means you are finally ready to toss aside these self-imposed shackles. With a little push, you can finally conquer your demons and claim the life you want.

Karina Says: If in doubt, remember this: fear kills more dreams than failure ever did.

Other Possible Meanings

- You are waiting for something to happen before making the changes you have promised yourself. Are you sure this is not just an excuse?
- Very occasionally, this card signifies someone is going to prison.

Meanings When Reversed

When the 8 of Swords is reversed, the scene is shaken up, and the woman is catapulted into action. New beginnings are possible now.

- You feel the fear and do it anyway. Go Team YOU!
- Restrictions are lifted. You are free to do what you want now.

9 of Swords: Feeling Anxious

Key Meaning: The 9 of Swords signifies that you feel anxious, and this anxiety is causing you sleepless nights.

The Card: The 9 of Swords presents a bleak picture. A woman sits alone in her bed crying. Notice the nine swords hanging ominously over her, like nightmares piercing her mind. When this card appears, you could be feeling worried, anxious, depressed, or lonely. The cause of your concern may be very real, like money, health or work problems. Or perhaps you have a decision hanging over you, which needs to be taken. Or maybe a relationship has gone wrong, or you are worried about a loved one. Then again, you may simply be anxious about what tomorrow will bring. When the 9 of Swords appears, it means things will not turn out as badly as you fear. The night plays tricks with the mind, casting shadows and making everything loom larger than life. You are gently guided to assess your worries in the light of day, perhaps even talk them over with someone. Your mind is creating monsters, and the best way to deal with monsters is to tackle them head-on. You may think of something you can do – an action you can take – which will at least make you feel more in control. Or more likely, you discover that the monster is only a little kitten and you've been worrying over things that really do not matter in the grander scheme of things.

Karina Says: Remember, no amount of regret can change the past, and no amount of anxiety can change the future. The only thing you can change is the thought you choose today. Our greatest weapon against worry is our ability to choose one thought over another.

Other Possible Meanings

- You are suffering from insomnia, hot flashes, or night sweats.
- You feel guilty about something you have done.
- Anxiety is habit-forming. Are you continually replacing one worry with the next?

In all cases, draw another card for guidance on what to do next.

Meanings When Reversed

Reversed, the woman appears on top of the picture, she is back in control.

- Worries come to an end. You are no longer plagued by anxiety.
- You or a loved one recover successfully from illness or surgery.
- You receive counselling or therapy which eases your mental and/or physical pain.

10 of Swords: Time To Let Go

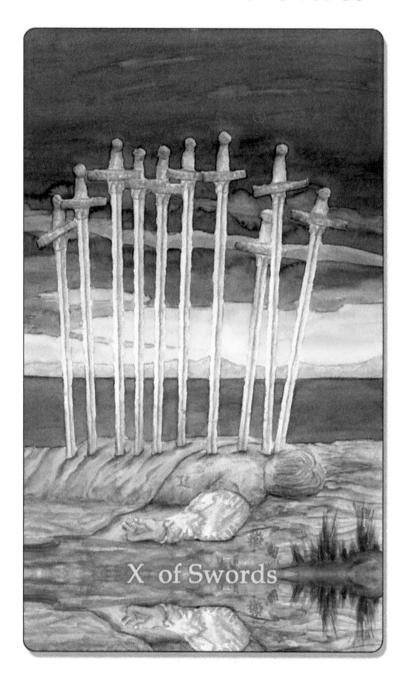

Key Meaning: The 10 of Swords ushers in a new era of major transformation. Be prepared to let go of your old life and habits.

The Card: At first, this may seem like a scary card, but trust me, it is not! In fact, it is rather exciting if you embrace the message. The lifeless body of a man lies in a desolate wasteland. He has been stabbed ten times in the back, to be sure to be sure! Clearly, he is not coming back to life! When the 10 of Swords appears, it indicates there is no life left in a matter or situation. This may be a welcome relief or, alternatively, cause you to feel unsettled. Major change is occurring, and whole areas of your life are being swept away. For example, you may lose a job or an important relationship, or a project or business could fail. As difficult as this is, whatever transpires now is forcing you in a new direction. Take note of the rising sun in the background of the card. This is meant to reassure you that a new dawn is approaching. As one cycle finishes, a new one can begin. You are certainly going through the process of psychological change and discovery. Expect your view of life and spirituality to change. Submit to the wind of change, because the more you cling on to rigid ideas of who you are, and how you should be treated, the more difficult you will find this period. Let go, and soar high. It is your karmic destiny to transform at this time.

Karina Says: Just when the caterpillar thought the world had come to an end, she became a butterfly.

Other Possible Meanings

- Accept the changes, even difficult ones. Embrace the new world order as it emerges.
- You are taking an interest in near-death experiences and the after-life. This is good.
- You have a stabbing back pain. Consider seeing an acupuncturist.

Meanings When Reversed

Reversed, we can view the sunrise more clearly. By now, you no longer have regrets and are ready to move on.

- Exciting new breakthroughs happen now.
- Recovery from illness.

Page of Swords: Unexpected News

Key Meaning: The Page of Swords signifies unexpected news. Or news which arrives sooner or later than you expect.

The Card: This young Page appears ready and alert. He clutches his sword with both hands, prepared to act on whatever news arrives. The storm clouds are gathering, cautioning him to remain vigilant. Expect the unexpected, this card warns. If you are waiting for news, it could come sooner or later than you expect. But don't worry, everything still works out for the best in the end. The Page also cautions you to keep your eyes peeled for an opportunity or idea which appears out-of-the-blue in the coming days or weeks. Pay attention when this happens because you could easily overlook something which otherwise could turn out to be quite spectacular.

Personality: When the Page refers to a person, he or she is young and a fast learner. They are quick-minded and good at turning situations to their advantage. They tend to be introverted, and choose their words wisely – some say they are insensitive to others feelings. Swords are associated with air signs in astrology, so this may represent an Aquarius, Gemini or Libra. Careers the Page of Sword are attracted to include: technical, scientific, law, design, accounting, and writing.

Karina Says: Impatience convinces us that everything has to happen now and exactly as we want it. Faith reassures us that everything happens when and how it is meant to.

Other Possible Meanings

- Have courage and communicate your ideas to others. Consider public speaking, writing, or creating video content on YouTube.

Meanings When Reversed

When the Page is reversed, the waiting is over. The opportunity arrives, or the news is delivered.

Knight of Swords: The Wait Is Over!

Key Meaning: The Knight of Swords signifies the wait is over. When this card appears, be prepared to move fast because life is about to get crazy!

The Card: The Knight charges full speed ahead on his horse. Dressed in armour, his red cape flapping in the wind, he races to your side, rescuing you from whatever it is that has been dragging you down. When this Knight arrives in your reading, hold on to your hat because life is about to get interesting. Delays are over, events take off, and you may have to take some speedy decisions. You could receive a job offer, for example. Or a project or business suddenly sparks into life. Maybe you move home, conceive or have a baby, or find a new lover. Trust that whatever happens now is the answer to your deepest desires; whether you know it or not!

Personality: When the Knight refers to a person, he is a young man (under 30) who is sporty and full of energy. Quick-minded, with a magnetic personality, he draws you in. As a lover, this Knight is great fun, and the chemistry is mind-blowing, *if you know wot I mean girls*. When the Knight is reversed, however, be on your guard because he is full of hot air; more of a one-night stand kind of guy. In astrology, swords are associated with air, so this may represent a Gemini, Libra, or Aquarius.

Karina Says: If you are waiting for the 'right time', it is now.

Other Possible Meanings

- You suddenly feel motivated and energised to achieve your goals.
- Someone is honest with you and holds nothing back. See this as a good thing.

Meanings When Reversed

When reversed, poor horsey lands on his head and the Knight has no way of moving forward.

- You experience delays, or issues arise which block your path.
- Are you holding back, not saying what you want to say? If so, now is the time to speak up.

Queen of Swords: You Should Inspire Others

Key Meaning: The Queen of Swords signifies you can inspire others with your words or actions.

The Card: The Queen sits on her high throne, holding a sword which faces up towards the heavens and higher truth. She reaches her hand out, directing our attention to something. When this card appears, it means you have something worth saying or teaching, possibly knowledge born of your experiences. You could choose writing, public speaking, social media, or event management as your outlet to reach a wider audience. Alternatively, you may prefer to focus on your local community. Maybe you are inspired to organise something to make a point. To show people there is a better way of doing things. Notice the lone bird approaching in the distance on this card. Traditionally, birds are considered messengers from the spirit world. This bird is about to drop an idea into your lap, so be prepared to listen. You are connecting to greater consciousness now, downloading ideas which are meant to be shared. This is a serious responsibility but one worthy of your crown.

Personality: When the Queen refers to a person, she is a strong woman, who is unpretentious and direct. She speaks plainly, even if her honesty is a little brutal at times. This Queen is kind at heart, but do not make the mistake of taking her for granted or worse – betraying her – because you will make an enemy for life. Rational to the point of appearing unemotional, she is just the person you want by your side in a crisis. Swords are associated with air signs in astrology, so this may represent an Aquarius, Gemini or Libra.

Karina Says: When you find the confidence to shine your light, you automatically inspire others to do the same.

Other Possible Meanings

- You have a talent for delivering messages from the 'other side'.

Meanings When Reversed

Reversed, the sword drops out of the Queen's hand, and she is less sure of what she wants to say. This is only a temporary state. Draw another card to discover how to resolve this impasse.

King of Swords: Step Into Your Power

King of Swords

Key Meaning: The King of Swords signifies it is time to step into your power and embrace your destiny.

The Card: The King sits on his throne, holding a sword which faces up towards the heavens and higher truth. He does not look very happy, does he? When this card appears, you may be resisting taking on a leadership role, perhaps in your career or another area of interest. Maybe you fear the work involved, or you lack faith in your abilities. Notice the two birds approaching in the distance. Traditionally birds are the messengers of the hidden world. They announce you are the vessel of a higher power, and you must rise to the occasion. Step into your power. But perhaps you are already doing this? If so, congratulations, this card acts as a confirmation that you are on the right path.

Personality: When the King refers to a person, he is usually a well-educated professional man. He is logical and offers good advice. Not the easiest of men to live with, however, he does like routines and set rules. Typically, he works in law, security, law enforcement, I.T., government, or the military. Swords are connected to astrology's air signs, so this may represent an Aquarius, Libra, or Gemini.

Karina Says: Waiting for people to like or approve of you, is a bit like handing them a gun to shoot you. Don't go there! Be confident and trust your intuition.

Other Possible Meanings

- Concern about being 'liked' or what others think is preventing you from moving forward.
- You should consult a professional about your problem, such as a doctor, lawyer, or plumber.

Meanings When Reversed

Reversed, the sword drops out of the King's hand, and he is less sure of himself.

- Your confusion is temporary. Draw another card for guidance on your next steps.

PENTACLES

Ace of Pentacles: Beginning of Prosperity

Key Meaning: The Ace of Pentacles signifies the beginning of financial prosperity. This is the card you want to see when applying for a job, bank loan, or area of study. Yes, you will be successful. Whatever you are inspired to focus on now, provides the key to your future security.

The Card: A path stretches out before you, with an archway at the end. The doorway lies open for you to walk through and begin a new life with fewer money concerns. All you need do is accept the opportunity, the shiny pentacle coming out of the cloud. Don't try to figure out where this may lead in the distant future; it is not possible to plan that far ahead. Rather, put one foot in front of the other and trust that you are setting off on a sparkling new path.

Karina Says: This card often turns up when we are confused about which direction to take in life, and suddenly a path appears. A doorway has opened, but it is still up to you to step through. Don't allow doubt or fear to stand in your way.

Other Possible Meanings

- A business, project, hobby, or investment idea you have is worth pursuing.
- You are successful in the sale/purchase of a property. Can also indicate a long-term let.
- Now is a good time to study, as this will increase your future earning potential.

Meanings When Reversed

When the card is reversed, the pentacle drops to the ground indicating a lost opportunity.

- Are you missing an opportunity? Look more closely at what is in front of you.
- There is an opportunity here to earn money 'under the table'.
- A financial settlement, investment return, or bonus may be less than expected.

2 of Pentacles: You Can Handle It!

Key Meaning: The 2 of Pentacles signifies you need to juggle various elements of your life at this time in order to achieve your goals. But don't worry, the juggler says you can handle it!

The Card: A juggler tosses two pentacles in the air, but there is little chance the coins will drop because they are bound by the ribbon of infinity. The light-hearted manner of the juggler reassures us that the situation is not dire. While you may be juggling various parts of your life – perhaps even exhausted by the effort – don't lose heart. It will all be worth it in the end.

Karina Says: The symbol of infinity encloses the pentacles and reminds us that life is an eternal cycle. We have up and down days; we cannot have one without the other. How would you recognise a 'good' day unless you have a 'bad' day to compare it with? There is no light unless there is darkness. Regardless of what's going on around you, accept there is a rhythm and this will ease any sense of impatience.

Other Possible Meanings

- You are juggling more than one job or project. Keep going because you are building a brighter future for yourself.
- Money is tight, and you may be robbing Peter to pay Paul. Things will ease soon.
- You are struggling to make a decision about something. Both options are good, so just choose one!

Meanings When Reversed

When the juggler is reversed, he struggles to balance the pentacles. This indicates you find all this multi-tasking too much.

- Consider doing less for now. As it happens, you'll probably end up achieving more.
- The need to multi-task is coming to an end. You will soon be able to narrow your focus.

3 of Pentacles: You Have Talent

III of Pentacles

Key Meaning: The 3 of Pentacles signifies recognition for your talent or skills. This is the card you want to see if you are hoping for positive feedback from others about something you are doing. Occasionally, it even means fame!

The Card: An artisan working on a church carving receives approval from two admirers as he finishes his artistic creation. His talent is appreciated but he is still the apprentice, fine-tuning his skills. When the 3 of Pentacles appears, it means, whatever it is you want from your working life – fame, money or job satisfaction – your goal is achievable. Continue on your path, because it is the right one, but you still have much to learn. As your star rises, try to keep your ego in check. Remain open to listening and learning from others.

Karina Says: Three is a magical number and represents the three elements of humankind: body, mind, and spirit. If you are going to spend a large portion of your life working, then at least ensure you enjoy it. A meaningless job will not feed your soul. If this card appears in your reading, it signifies you have the ability to inspire others through your actions, words, and deeds.

Other Possible Meanings

- You receive an award, bonus, or promotion for your efforts.
- You receive help from a new mentor who helps you progress.

Meanings When Reversed

When the artisan is reversed, the tools fall out of his hands. This means you feel unprepared or disillusioned.

- Don't give up too easily. You have God-given talents.
- A reward or bonus is not forthcoming this time. Try again.
- You may receive some criticism if your work is being assessed. Learn what you can.

4 of Pentacles: Money Flows To You

IV of Pentacles

Key Meaning: The 4 of Pentacles signifies the flow of money coming to you. This money is reward for your work and efforts to date. Great news! You are building a bright future and are on the path to long-term financial security.

The Card: A man clutches the pentacles he has worked hard to acquire. In the background is the city where he lives and works successfully. The 4 of Pentacles is particularly affected by other cards around it. Draw another card for more guidance. If the card is positive, then you are building a firm foundation for the future and should be proud of your efforts. If it is negative, this acts as a warning not to become so attached to achievement and material gain that you become unsympathetic or greedy.

Karina Says: You receive money in return for the energy you expend in work. It is not a 'necessary evil', as some would say. Money has a place in this physical world; you are body, as well as mind and spirit. It is worthy to want financial security in order to take care of yourself and those you love. How you earn your money and what you spend it on, however... now, therein is your soul's opportunity to shine.

Other Possible Meanings

- This is a good time to start a pension or long-term saving plan.
- The Universe is blessing you with good fortune; be sure to share it with others.
- Occasionally, this card means you will feel more energetic when you lose weight.

Meanings When Reversed

Reversed, the pentacles drop out of your hands, indicating problems holding on to money.

- Careful; you are spending too much, or spending your money on the wrong things.
- Consider new ways to earn more money.

V of Pentacles

Key Meaning: The 5 of Pentacles is probably one of the most depressing cards in the Tarot. It indicates hard times, such as experiencing financial problems, losing a job, home, or income support. Occasionally, it warns of illness or depression.

The Card: Two lost souls stumble past a brightly-lit church. Inside is salvation, but they do not stop to look and seek a solution to their problems. Perhaps the expensively ornate window makes them feel hard done by, as though everyone else is lucky except them. When the 5 of Pentacles appears, you may have suffered a loss or disappointment. You can always draw another card to indicate the cause of your difficulty if you are not sure what it is. Help is available once you are ready to move forward again. Just be careful not to overlook an opportunity that is right under your nose. Remember, focus on finding the solution to your situation rather than wallowing in the problem.

Karina Says: It may seem as though you can only move one step at a time. And that is fine. Be gentle with yourself as you move forward. Have faith and remember the darkest hour is just before dawn.

Other Possible Meanings

- You are finding it difficult to motivate yourself. Draw another card for guidance on how best to bring back the sparkle.
- Are you blaming others for your misfortunes? Perhaps it is time to take responsibility for the role you play in your life. This is not about allocating blame, but rather about self-empowerment.
- Are you depressed about the ending of a relationship? Let it go; you were looking for love in the wrong place.

Meanings When Reversed

This is one of the few tarot cards where a reversal is a serious cause for celebration!

- Finally, there is light at the end of the tunnel. You are moving past problems.
- Well-paid work appears after a period of unemployment or low paying jobs.
- Your health and emotional well-being improve.

6 of Pentacles: You Receive A Bonus

VI of Pentacles

Key Meaning: The 6 of Pentacles signifies you are about to receive a bonus, usually in the form of money. This may be dividends, an inheritance, work bonus, legal settlement, perhaps even a lottery win! When the pay-out arrives, it is generous.

The Card: An expensively dressed man donates money to the poor. In one hand, he has a bunch of coins and in the other hand a scale, indicating that the pay-out is fair. What comes to you now is well-deserved. Notice how the card looks different depending who you focus on. Intuitively, our eye tends to land on the character we sense has news for us. If the rich man catches your attention, he has news of money or assistance coming your way. If you are captivated by the poor souls at his feet, then you may soon have an opportunity to share your gift, time, or money with others.

Karina Says: Any good fortune you receive now is payback for past suffering and good deeds. The Book of Karma always keeps count. What goes around comes around, creating a cycle of fairness, equality, and justice.

Other Possible Meanings

- You are, or soon will be, in a position to help others. What you give now returns ten-fold to you in the future.

Meanings When Reversed

Reversed, the scale in the man's hands is no longer balanced. While you still receive a pay-out, it is less spectacular than it could have been.

- Gifts, investment payouts, bonuses or inheritances are smaller than expected.
- Money arrives, but there are strings attached.
- A get rich quick scheme backfires.

7 of Pentacles: Almost There!

Key Meaning: The 7 of Pentacles signifies you are almost there! All your hard work is about to pay off, so keep going! Now is not the time to give up.

The Card: A hard-working farmer stops to assess his handiwork. Six pentacles are planted, but one remains telling us there is still more to be done before he can enjoy the fruits of his labour. It may be that a project has absorbed all your time and energy, and you have yet to see the results. As tempting as it may be to quit, you must not. Your mission is to finish what you started; dedicate yourself to the task at hand and soon you will be able to claim your well-deserved bounty.

Karina Says: So often we give up too easily, and then bemoan how nothing works out for us. This little farmer reminds us that any worthy goal takes time and persistence to bear fruit. Have pride in what you are doing, and remember the journey is just as important as the destination.

Other Possible Meanings

- Finish what you started.
- Take a moment to acknowledge how far you have come. You are a star!
- This is a good time to reflect on what you should do next.

Meanings When Reversed

When the 7 of Pentacles is reversed, the coins drop away. Your hard work is not recognised or rewarded as it should be.

- You do not receive the reward/bonus/recognition you deserve.
- Someone steals your idea.
- Investments do not yield as much as you expect.
- Beware of impatience and rushing to the end.

Consider drawing another card for guidance; perhaps it is possible to prevent this outcome.

8 of Pentacles: Reward and Recognition

Key Meaning: The 8 of Pentacles signifies reward and recognition for your efforts. This could be a promotion, job offer, bonus, or award.

The Card: You are seen here as the master craftsman at work. Clever you! People have noticed your efforts and abilities, which could result in some sort of reward. But wait, look at the card! There is still a pentacle lying on the floor. This means more opportunities for advancement are yet to come, so don't relax your efforts. Have faith in your abilities because you have the potential to go right to the top. Whatever your situation in life, dream big.

Karina Says: This is a beautiful card to receive if you secretly wish to make a difference in the world. Think of yourself as a master builder, building something special with each tap of the hammer. Trust your path, even if you don't yet understand the bigger picture.

Other Possible Meanings

- You win/receive an award for your work.
- If you are taking exams, don't worry. You will pass with flying colours!

Meanings When Reversed

Reversed, the tools fall out of the craftsman's hands making the work more difficult and less enjoyable.

- Are you enjoying your work? If not, ask yourself: *Is it a dead-end job* or *Am I simply not putting my heart into it?*
- If you are lacking career direction, draw another card for guidance.
- Avoid the temptation to copy someone else's work. Trust your own originality.

9 of Pentacles: Financial Freedom

Key Meaning: The 9 of Pentacles promises serious financial gain; the sort of money and success which provides you with the freedom to spend your days as you want.

The Card: A beautifully-dressed woman stands in her blooming garden holding a falcon. There is an air of luxury and pleasure as she enjoys the taste of success. This happy card indicates you are at a point of achievement in your life where financial freedom is possible. Property and land are key here; you may have enough wealth to secure a beautiful home or long-term income. Appreciate your blessings, you have earned them. However, be careful not to become too self-indulgent and lose your edge. Outside the walls of this Eden still lies a competitive world. There are coded warnings in the card to keep your guard up: the protective glove the woman is wearing, the hood over the bird's head, and the lowly snail in the foreground who could chomp his way through your luscious pentacles.

Karina Says: Karma is paying you back now for all the times in life when you were not rewarded. Financial success and happiness are yours to enjoy but be aware that it is important to share this positive energy and abundance with others.

Other Possible Meanings

- You receive an inheritance, usually land or property.
- You earn enough to retire with financial security.
- You move to a new home or make home improvements.
- Your plan to work from home is successful.

Meanings When Reversed

Reversed, the garden appears disorganised and unkempt. It means there may be delays to plans while you get your house in order.

- There is a delay in receiving your financial windfall.
- Are you neglecting your home or garden? A beautiful environment is important to your emotional wellbeing.
- Occasionally means damage to the home caused by a storm.

10 of Pentacles: Good Fortune
For The Whole Family

Key Meaning: The 10 of Pentacles predicts your family's fortune is on the up and up. This is the card you want to see if you are hoping for great success and prosperity, not just for yourself but your whole family.

The Card: Everything is wonderful when this card turns up! The 10 of Pentacles promises wealth and happiness for the entire family. A wealthy old man sits in the foreground, his children and grandchild nearby. Where the previous card – the 9 of Pentacles – heralds enough money to support yourself, the 10 of Pentacles suggests enough wealth to support a family, perhaps even for generations to come.

Karina Says: The people we love deserve the best we have to offer. Sometimes, we unthinkingly take our frustrations out at home while reserving our smile for strangers. Be kind to your loved ones because they provide the emotional foundation you need to be successful.

Other Possible Meanings

- You receive an inheritance, or a long-term investment matures.
- You move to a new home/location where you settle for many years.
- A family business or project is successful.
- You are caring for elderly or sick relatives and receive reward or support for your efforts.

Meanings When Reversed

Reversed, the pentacles are now on the floor, and the family is 'up in the air'.

- The family is squabbling over money and inheritances.
- You are getting divorced and dividing family assets.
- Is someone neglecting their elderly parent's needs?
- Are you frittering away an inheritance? Be careful to save some for the future.

Page of Pentacles: News of an Offer

Page of Pentacles

Key Meaning: The Page of Pentacles signifies news of an offer is on the way! Depending on your situation, it could indicate a job or study opportunity, an award or something else that advances your life purpose.

The Card: This Page typically delivers good news of a practical matter, such as a job offer, college placement, or award. In this card, we see a young person holding a pentacle and – in the distance – a ploughed field waits to be planted. The field signifies that whatever opportunity or news arrives now, has the potential to mature into something much bigger and brighter in the future.

Personality: When the Page refers to a person, he or she is young, has little money but great prospects for the future. They are studious, hardworking, and have a sense of duty to family and the community. In astrology, pentacles are associated with earth signs, so this may represent a Capricorn, Taurus, or Virgo.

Karina Says: You have natural talent but even the gifted need to put in the work. Realise, the only thing that stands between you and true greatness – is you! Are you willing to make the necessary sacrifice? I hope so, because the world is waiting for you.

Other Possible Meanings

- You begin to study something which provides future earning possibilities.
- If you are waiting for legal paperwork – like a contract, court settlement, passport, or travel visa – you receive it shortly.

Meanings When Reversed

Reversed, the pentacle falls out of the Page's hand. This can indicate news is delayed.

- You experience a delay; the offer does not come through as quickly as you expect.
- Re-focus your attention on work or study. Your attention has been scattered.

Knight of Pentacles: You Are Making Steady Progress

Key Meaning: The Knight of Pentacles indicates you are making steady progress with your life. It may feel like you are stuck in a rut, because the pace is slow, but you are moving forward all the same. Events may even pick up speed now.

The Card: The Knight sits on his workhorse, surveying the pentacle in his hand and the fields to be ploughed. He is not rushing into action, but calmly pacing what needs to be done. When he appears, he says: *expect steady progress rather than overnight success.* What you commit to now – be that an investment, job, study or relationship – allow it time to flourish at a sensible pace.

Person: When the Knight refers to a person, he is a young man (under 30) who is loyal, keeps his word, and does a good job. He is solid, always willing to help, loves animals, nature and children. Some may consider him dull in love, but this Knight has a sensual, healthy lust for life. Pentacles are associated with earth signs in astrology, so this may represent a Capricorn, Taurus, or Virgo.

Karina Says: There is a misguided notion that if something is *meant to be*, then there will be no obstacles in the way. This is simply not true; obstacles are there to strengthen our resolve and shape our vision. Too many people quit too easily, only then to search furiously for a new dream, and repeat the cycle all over again. Listen to your heart, follow your desire, and don't give up.

Other Possible Meanings

- An opportunity for business travel arises, this may be expected or unexpected.
- You move location, perhaps even to another country.
- Your financial investments are sound and will rise steadily in value.

Meanings When Reversed

When reversed, our handsome Knight falls off his horse and is confused and unfocused. This causes a delay to plans, or progress is slower than expected.

- Has your confidence been temporarily knocked by events? If so, coax yourself back onto the saddle and grab the reins of your dream tightly.
- You experience delays in getting the job/promotion/award you hoped for.
- A project is successfully completed. Now you can take a break!

Queen of Pentacles: Time For Action

Key Meaning: The Queen of Pentacles indicates that now is the time for action. Do not wait for life to happen *to you*; start implementing improvements today.

The Card: The Queen of Pentacles gazes down at the pentacle in her hands. Her throne is surrounded by flowers and hills forming a practical, earthly connection. When she appears, she advises you to spend less time daydreaming and more time *doing*. There is no need for big changes at this time; instead, think steady progress on a daily basis. Create a solid environment for yourself at home and at work.

Person: When the Queen refers to a person, she is a strong woman with a cheerful attitude. She is not afraid of hard work and is good at business. More practical than idealistic, she loves a beautiful home and garden, takes care of her appearance, enjoys cooking and caring for the family. Pentacles are connected to the earth signs in astrology, so this may represent a Virgo, Taurus, or Capricorn.

Karina Says: At this time, spiritual enlightenment comes through what you *do*, rather than reflection.

Other Possible Meanings

- An opportunity presents itself which could improve your standard of living.
- As a natural carer, you will find satisfaction in a service-based career.

Meanings When Reversed

Reversed, our Queen is disorientated and forgets how magnificent she is.

- You are neglecting your appearance and/or environment (home, family, and friends).
- You feel your efforts are never good enough.

Fortunately, this is only a temporary state, and with a little time, you regain your throne.

King of Pentacles:
Significant Achievement

Key Meaning: The King of Pentacles indicates significant achievement. You have, or you will soon achieve, some major goals.

The Card: The King of Pentacles sits on his throne surrounded by riches and abundance. When he appears, he usually delivers news of worldly success, where the Queen of Pentacles can signify success in any practical area (home, family, study, or work). At this time, you have the Midas touch, everything you touch turns to gold. Although it may seem to outsiders that you are lucky, they don't see the endless hours you devote to work while they are wasting time. Enjoy your success – you deserve it.

Person: When the King refers to a person, he is a mature man of solid character, a pillar of the family and community. Tough in business but kind at heart. Prosperous, resourceful, usually a land/property owner. He may work in finance, banking, building, or with animals. Some say this King is boring but, in a crisis, he is the man you want by your side. In astrology, pentacles are associated with earth signs, so he may represent a Virgo, Capricorn, or Taurus.

Karina Says: Money can raise us up – we can use it to build something of beauty and value, and share our good fortune with others. Or it can drag us down; it can tease out our worst traits, like the desire to show off. Money is not the root of all evil; it is simply a tool to test our character.

Other Possible Meanings

- This is a good time to invest in property or shares.
- You receive a lifetime achievement award or significant public recognition.

Meanings When Reversed

When reversed, the King's values are upside-down. This is a warning not to let success go to your head. Ask yourself:

- Am I acting superior to others or obsessed with status?
- Do my values and actions truly reflect the greatness of my spirit?

SPREADS

ADVANCED READINGS

Let's Try Some 3-Card Spreads!

When you want to shake things up, try these three-card spreads for guidance. Shuffle the cards and count to ten as normal. Stop and take the top three cards when you finish.

Spread 1: Ask a Question

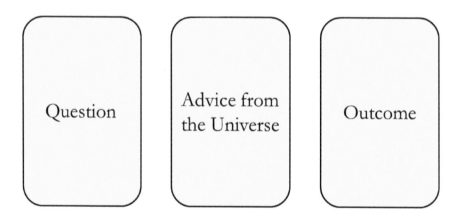

Card 1: Ask the Tarot your question. The card you receive in this spot should reflect the nature of your question. If it does not, then it means the Tarot wants to talk about another issue first.

Card 2: What the Universe advises you to do.

Card 3: How things will turn out, if you follow the guidance of card 2.

Example

Question: What should I focus on now?

Card 1: Tower

"The Tower strips away any false sense of security, in the home, relationships, work, belief system or sense of self. It may even feel like the Universe is 'out to get you', as events come with speed, one thing after the other. The problems cannot be dodged but must be faced and dealt with."

Yikes – be prepared to deal with some major changes in your life. Whatever part of your life is disrupted now, is where you should focus your attention. The Tower is a Major Arcana card, and when it appears, it forces a much-needed shake-up, paving the way to magical new beginnings.

Advice from the Universe

Card 2: 5 of Wands

"The 5 of Wands indicates you need to be prepared to fight for what you want. All it takes is a little courage and staying power."

Be prepared to move out of your comfort zone in the months ahead; the only way we can benefit from change is to go through change. Put one foot in front of the other and march forward.

Outcome

Card 3: Judgement

"You are seeing the world with fresh eyes, as though you are waking from a slumber. You begin to see solutions to problems which have evaded you in the past; worries evaporate and appear smaller on the scale of things after this new awakening."

The Judgement card reassures that any difficulties you encounter now, will lead to greater clarity and a sense of purpose in the future. Then, you can move full speed ahead.

Spread 2: What Am I Missing?

What is missing in my life?	What is the first step to achieving it?	Then what happens?

Card 1: Ask the Tarot, what is missing in your life.

Card 2: What step should you take to remedy the situation?

Card 3: What happens if you follow the guidance of card 2?

Example

This is a reading I gave to a client of mine. She is a talented healer but is afraid to use her gift out of fear of being ridiculed.

What is missing in my life?

Card 1: King of Swords

"The King of Swords signifies it is time to step into your power and embrace your destiny."

A clear message. She must overcome her fear and embrace her destiny. She will not be happy until she does so. Sometimes it may seem like we have a choice, but it only *seems* that way. The Universe will find a million ways to force you down the path you are supposed to follow. You may as well go for it!

What is the first step to achieving it?

Card 2: The Lovers

The Lovers signifies having a passion for what you do. Passion doesn't appear out of thin air; it is the by-product of effort and hard work. This client is advised to throw herself into her healing career, and her enthusiasm will provide a natural antidote to fear. The Lovers also means a choice has to be made. She must go *all in* or walk away. Nothing is ever achieved by half methods.

Then what happens?

Card 3: The Sun

Happiness, positivity, and a sense of purpose is her reward. The Sun is the ultimate success card. Emerge from the shadows and step into the spotlight. This is a reminder that nothing much is ever achieved when we hide away. Experiment with your life, do what you feel inclined to do, and express your uniqueness. Dazzle us all.

Spread 3: Love

What I feel about him/her	What he/she feels about me	Do we have a future?

Card 1: What do you really feel about the person?
Card 2: How do they really feel about you?
Card 3: Do you have a future?

Example
This reading was for a client who was very unhappy in her marriage.

What do I feel about him?
Card 1: Ace of Swords

Swords rule communication; they often appear when someone is struggling to express their feelings. In this case, the client really wants to open up to her husband and tell him that she no longer loves him. But she is scared by the prospect of divorce and change. The Ace of Swords indicates that an opportunity will occur for her to talk and she should take it.

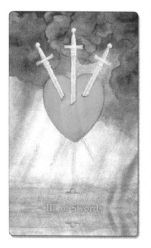

What he feels about me
Card 2: 3 of Swords

This card has a picture of a heart, cut by three swords. The heart is a universal symbol of love, and when it is cut, there is a release of emotions – hurt, pain, grief, and a sense of loss. It seems her husband is also feeling estranged and lonely in the marriage. This surprised the client; because she was so focused on her own feelings, she had not seriously considered that her husband might feel the same way.

Do we have a future?
Card 3: 10 of Swords

The 10 of Swords represents the end of a situation. It is likely, looking at these cards, when both parties are honest about their feelings, neither will wish to continue in the marriage. Rather than allow the sadness to drift on, they bring their relationship to an end, freeing each other to find love elsewhere. There is a great sense of relief and finality with the 10 of Swords.

Spread 4: Life Purpose

What is my life purpose?	What talent am I overlooking?	What should I focus on now?

Card 1: What is your life purpose?

Card 2: What natural talent or skill are you overlooking?

Card 3: What action should you focus on now, that will help you live your life purpose?

Example

What is my life purpose?

Card 1: The Chariot

When this card appears, it means where there has been stagnation in your life, there is now movement. It tells us that you have already been actively fulfilling your life purpose, perhaps through a job or hobby, but maybe you walked away or questioned it because things did not turn out as you expected. The Chariot represents triumph over obstacles, and guides you to recommit and focus.

What talent am I overlooking?

Card 2: Knight of Pentacles

A very interesting card to follow the Chariot. You are not overlooking a talent, but impatience is impeding the development of your talent. The Knight of Pentacles represents slow and steady progress, rather than overnight success. You are guided not to be put off by the obstacles in your path. Most people achieve things, not because they are born geniuses, but because they have practised or apprenticed for thousands of hours.

What should I focus on now?

Card 3: Ace of Pentacles

An opportunity presents itself, or soon will. There is a risk you could overlook this opportunity because of past disappointments. Notice a path in the picture which leads out of the garden into unknown territory. You are invited to take a risk and step through the archway. Prosperity is the reward on the other side but, be under no illusion, the path will be long and require patience and persistence to navigate. Have faith in your ability. The Universe only delivers opportunities we are capable of rising to. Seize the moment.

SAMPLE READING

LESSONS

Master Lesson

In this Master Lesson section, I will show you how I interpret different cards, in response to the same question. Each example contains a little lesson on how to improve your card reading abilities, helping you become the awesome Tarot reader everyone wants to know!

Question 1: Will I find love?

Card You Receive: Ace of Cups

The Ace of Cups has several meanings, but when you ask specifically about love and receive this joyful card, then the answer is clear. Yes! A new love is about to enter your life. In fact, the Ace of Cups is considered the ultimate love card, a wonderful omen. Notice the cup overflowing with water. Water represents our deepest desires, and the cup on offer promises to deliver in abundance. This relationship will turn out to be very important and most likely lead to serious commitment and marriage.

Question 2: Will I find love?

Card You Receive: Judgement

The first thing to note is that Judgement is part of the Major Arcana and because of this it is a powerful destiny card. It heralds the resurrection of an old situation, which is why Archangel Gabriel blows his trumpet to awaken the dead. What was once considered *dead* or in the past, springs back into life. As you asked about love, this could mean an old flame re-appears on the scene; you may get back with an ex-, or you might meet someone new who *feels* familiar, like you have known each other before (most likely you have but in a past life).

When a destiny card turns up in your reading, it means fate has led you to this point. Perhaps you are worried; wondering if you have taken a wrong turn in life. You have not. Your experiences helped shape the person you are today, the person you needed to become in order to attract this powerful relationship, and more importantly – maintain it. So, relax, trust, and wait for lightning to strike!

Question 3: Will I find love?

Card You Receive: 9 of Swords

You ask about love, and you get the 9 of Swords! No cups or message of love in sight. Confusing isn't it. When a card does not appear to answer your question, it is the Tarot's way of saying 'I want to talk about another issue first, because it impacts your question'. In this case, the 9 of Swords refers to your emotional state. It suggests you are feeling low or stressed out. The card gently whispers, *Take care of yourself first. This is not the best time to attract love.* Although it is tempting to believe the excitement of finding a new love will solve everything, it rarely does. Rather, we end up settling for less than our true worth, because our confidence is low. In this instance, the 9 of Swords guides you to heal. Find balance and deal with the real problems which are causing you to feel this way. When you are done, you will light up like a beacon and attract the love you deserve.

Question 4: Will I find love?

Card You Receive: Ace of Pentacles

You ask about love, and you receive the Ace of Pentacles. Unlike the Ace of Cups, this Ace is not a traditional love card. It is related more to practical actions than matters of the heart. So, what could the Tarot mean by this? It is saying a practical action is necessary, in order to set in motion the sequence of events which will lead you to meet your true love. This action is likely to be something you are already thinking about doing; for example, changing jobs, starting a business, undertaking a new course or hobby, or moving location. In this instance, the Tarot is guiding you to act; to shake things up. Perhaps you instinctively know this already? Listen to your instincts. Not only will you find love, but you will also discover a whole new world.

Note: This could equally apply to the Ace of Wands; if you received the Ace of Wands, you would simply be guided by the actions associated with that card.

Question 5: Will I find love?

Card You Receive: Queen of Pentacles

You ask about love, and you receive the Queen of Pentacles, a court (personality) card. If you are searching for a female lover, then this reading is straightforward – it represents the person you will fall in love with. But what if you are looking for a male? Then, it is more confusing, isn't it? In that case, take it to mean the Queen is you. You may or may not identify with the personality traits of the Queen of Pentacles, but you are guided to look at her picture. She looks content, doesn't she? Happy with her life and achievements? Wonderful! You may even wonder how serious is this happy woman about finding love. Life seems pretty fulfilling already. Maybe she is surrounded with enough love, from parents, family, children, friends, or pets. The Tarot wants you to know that it is OK to be single and enjoy your freedom. Do not feel pressured into settling down because you feel you 'should'. You are not like other people; you are unique. It does not mean you have to stay single forever. Far from it! When and if your needs change, you will have no problem finding a partner.

Question 6: Do we have a future?

Card You Receive: 10 of Cups

The 10 of Cups is known as the happy-ever-after card. The meaning is clear, yes, you do have a happy future with the person you asked about. Isn't it lovely when the answer is so straightforward! Tarot reflects life. There are times when we *know* with certainty what we must do or where our destiny lies. The Tarot will reflect these moments of clarity. While life can be messy and complicated, just sometimes it manages to be beautifully simple.

Question 7: Do we have a future?

Card You Receive: Temperance

The first thing to note is that Temperance is a Major Arcana and, thus, a powerful destiny card. Archangel Michael pours water from one cup to another, a symbolic act of renewing energy. As Temperance traditionally refers to healing, it signifies that your relationship is going through a healing process. It may be a joint healing, or that one of you is acting as an angel, helping the other to renew. As Temperance is a destiny card, it means this relationship – as well as the healing process – was part of your destiny. There is a big karmic lesson involved; no running away from this one! It is easy to enjoy a person in good times, less so in hard times. And yet, think of a squadron of soldiers, how bonded they become by experiencing difficult times together. You are forming a bond which will endure a lifetime.

Question 8: Do we have a future?

Card You Receive: 7 of Cups

As we know, cups reflect emotions. The 7 of Cups, therefore, must have something to do with emotions. However, this card is confusing because it does not seem to answer your question directly, does it? Look at the woman in the card; she seems overwhelmed by all the cups and unsure where to focus her attention. When a card does not specifically answer your question, it is the Tarot's way of guiding you to ponder a different question. Could it be that your problem is not really about love after all, but something else? Maybe, like the woman in the card, you are confused by life at this time and uncertain what will make you happy. It is easy to fixate on a relationship as being the problem, or even to fantasise that a new relationship might provide a solution. In reality, the problem more often lies within ourselves, and not with someone else. A sense of dissatisfaction is best addressed by bringing more meaning to your day, by focusing on *doing* something that will give you a greater sense of purpose and satisfaction. Pick one thing you enjoy doing and move forward! This will help you find greater happiness within yourself and, as a result, in your relationship.

Question 9: Do we have a future?

Card You Receive: 4 of Pentacles

You ask about love, and you receive the 4 of Pentacles. This card does not seem to have anything to do with relationships. Or does it? Take a look at the picture. A man clutches his coins tightly; these coins represent his money, security, possessions, and property. Could it be that you are clinging to your relationship for security, or practical reasons, like money, kids, or property? Or, maybe you are attracted to someone because of the 'things' they can provide you with? No-one likes to believe such things of themselves, but it is human nature to take the easier path. As the 4 of Pentacles represents holding on for dear life, it means your relationship status will remain the same. No-one leaves, but no-one seeks to change or improve either.

Remember, the 4 of Pentacles is a Minor Arcana card – which means the future it predicts is not set in stone. You can always alter the future by changing your actions today. The beauty of Tarot is that it can show you an alternative path if you are willing to listen and, more importantly, act. Simply draw another card for guidance.

Question 10: Do we have a future?

Card You Receive: Tower

You ask about love, and receive one of the most powerful 'change' cards in Tarot. This Major Arcana card often turns up when we have been craving change but not found the motivation or courage to instigate it. The Tower strips away a sense of security, laying your relationship bare for all to see. No more pretending or ignoring issues. I have seen this card turn up for affairs exposed, uncomfortable truths being told, or lies uncovered. Whatever happens now may be uncomfortable, and turn your world upside down. One fine day, however, you will realise it was exactly the shakeup you needed to regain your happiness in the longer term.

Question 11: Will I start a new job this year?

Card You Receive: Sun

When the Sun turns up, the answer is inevitably yes! Furthermore, the new opportunity will turn out spectacularly well. As a Major Arcana card, the Sun means it is your destiny at this time to move forward in your career. It may be that this job is a stepping stone to greater opportunities or the conduit to you meeting new people who are fated to be part of your future. You do not need to know the details, only that the guidance is clear. Start applying for jobs if you have not already done so! Trust your instincts, Higher powers communicate to us through our feelings and instincts. You were guided to ask this question for a reason.

Question 12: Will I start a new job this year?

Card You Receive: King of Swords

Personality cards can be difficult to interpret in readings, which is why I have provided more specific meanings with *Tarot in 5 Minutes*. The King of Swords, as you will see, often appears when someone is 'resisting taking on a leadership role.' As this card does not provide a specific answer to your question, we must take it to mean that the Tarot wishes to raise another matter first. It may be that you lack confidence in your abilities, and are settling for less than your true worth. Maybe you are worried about applying for a promotion or job upgrade because you are not sure you have what it takes. Until you step into your power, nothing much will change. This card comes as a reminder that you are ready. So, feel the fear and do it anyway! You may also find that your new boss has the characteristics of the King of Swords.

Question 13: Will I start a new job this year?

Card You Receive: 5 of Wands

You ask about work, and you receive the 5 of Wands. When you read the meaning of the 5 of Wands, it says 'be prepared to fight for what you want.' So, does that mean you will start a new job? No, not necessarily. The 5 of Wands is a Minor Arcana card, which means free will and not destiny is at play here. Your actions – what you do now – will shape the outcome of this question. If you want a new job, you are going to have to compete for it and perform well in the interview. The good news is, you are more than capable of achieving what you want; you just need to want it enough to make it happen.

Question 14: Will I move location?

Card You Receive: Knight of Pentacles

The Knight of Pentacles has several meanings, but when you ask specifically about moving, and he turns up, then the answer to your question is yes. Knights always represent movement, usually after a period of delay or stagnation. You will also get an idea of timing by looking at the picture of the plodding Knight. He does not look in a hurry, does he? Compare this, for example, to the Knight of Swords who can be seen racing into action. The Knight of Pentacles represents a calm and steady pace, so your move will not happen overnight. In comparison, if you were to receive the Knight of Swords, I'd advise you to start packing now!

Question 15: Will I move location?

Card You Receive: 5 of Cups

You ask about moving, and you receive the 5 of Cups. This card represents feeling sad about recent or past events, but that does not really answer your question, does it!? When this happens, it may well be that your heart was not seriously invested in the question. Something else is occupying your mind, and *that* is what the Tarot wants to talk about. The best way to handle this situation is to thank the Tarot, and say, 'OK, please let me know what you want to say about my sadness,' and then pick another card.

Question 16: Will I move location?

Card You Receive: 5 of Pentacles

Occasionally, we need a reminder that the Tarot is not a magic genie. It does not have the power to solve our problems with the turn of a card. We may turn to the Tarot in desperation, hoping it will predict a lottery windfall which solves all our problems. So, when we receive a bit of a downer card, like the 5 of Pentacles, it can be disappointing. No-one wants to read about hard times, or wishes unfulfilled, and yet – struggle is part of the ebb and flow of life. As with all Minor Arcana cards, remember the outcome is not set in stone. If you would like to move house, then ask the Tarot how to bring this about. The important thing is, you must be prepared to listen and act, even if it requires a massive effort to move out of your comfort zone. It is only by punching through our challenges that we get to experience the best days of our lives.

Question 17: Will I move location?

Card You Receive: Page of Wands

You ask about moving, and receive the Page of Wands. If you read the meaning of this card, it does not refer specifically to moving but the arrival of good news. So, ask yourself – how could this fit my situation? Maybe you are on a waiting list for a home and finally hear back. Or you hear about a mortgage you applied for, house sale, or job which facilitates a relocation. Wands represent action; practical steps which take you closer to achieving your dream. When a personality (court) card turns up in answer to a relocation question, it is worth looking at the card for additional visual clues about where you could move to. Perhaps the personality is pointing in a particular direction, or there is a river, tree, or mountain which reminds you of a particular place. There will not always be a clue, but if there is meant to be one, it will stick out like a sore thumb, and you'll wonder why you had never noticed that particular element in the card before.

Question 18: How can I improve my health?

Card You Receive: 3 of Wands

You asked about health, and receive the 3 of Wands. This card does not seem to have much to do with health, does it? Traditionally, it indicates help is on the way – notice the ships arriving in the distance. While this could mean someone is about to offer you advice or aid, you must consider the question posed: *How* can I improve my health? You are asking the Tarot what action *you* can take. So, while help may well be on the way, the Tarot is also guiding you to take a specific action. Remember, wands are all about action. It could be that you are being advised to search for answers overseas (travel or via the internet). As this is the 3 of wands, rather than an Ace (fresh ideas), it is likely that an idea has already occurred to you.

Question 19: How can I improve my health?

Card You Receive: Tower

The Tower is a Major Arcana card which indicates that you have asked an important question and the Tarot wants to provide guidance. The Tower can be scary, as it heralds a sudden change in circumstances. Think of it as a wake-up call; the Universe's way of saying – take control and make the necessary lifestyle changes you need to, or fate will force the changes on you. This is not a time for half measures. If you need to lose weight, quit smoking, drink less alcohol, or reduce stress, try to make your health goals a priority. Sometimes we need a little Cosmic push; consider this to be one of those times.

Question 20: How can I improve my health?

Card You Receive: 8 of Pentacles

The 8 of Pentacles is associated with reward and recognition at work, so how could this relate to your health? Remember, the Tarot is limited to 78 cards and has to try somehow to convey a specific, personal message to you. Study the picture in the card; what could it be saying? We see a man, working diligently, in a focused manner. He is not over-worked (as in the 10 of Wands). He looks happy, and there is a sense of achievement about his day.

Research shows that satisfaction (and ultimately happiness) comes from achievement; in sticking to something and seeing it through. The guidance here is to apply yourself in a meaningful way to doing something that gives you a sense of achievement, and do not be surprised if those aches and pains subsequently fade away.

Question 21: How can I make more money?

Card You Receive: The Emperor

The Emperor is a Major Arcana card which means your question is an important one to address at this time. The Emperor talks of ambition and encourages you to believe you can achieve more with your life. He guides you to push yourself, study, or work in a more focused and productive way. He is not advising you on a specific path, but rather to adopt a can-do attitude. This is a much bigger issue than money or paying bills; it is about you and what you are doing with your time on earth. If you want more, then you must accept the lead role in this play called My Life.

Question 22: How can I make more money?

Card You Receive: 3 of Cups

You ask about money, and receive the 3 of Cups. This card typically means 'cause for celebration.' This answer might make more sense if you had asked, *Will I get the promotion?* However, as you wanted to know – *how* can I make more money – we must dig a little deeper to understand what the Tarot is trying to say. Look at the girls' dancing, drinking, and enjoying each other's company. What type of job does this conjure up to you? It could be you are guided to consider event management, wedding planning, entertainment, hospitality, or even a business which supplies gifts for happy occasions. The 3 of Cups also represents spending time with other people, so it could be that opportunities will appear through networking.

Question 23: How can I make more money?

Card You Receive: 4 of Swords

You ask about money, and receive the 4 of Swords, which means time to rest. In other words, the Tarot is not answering your question directly, but raising another issue. Perhaps you have been very busy, stressed out, or are recovering from illness or surgery. This is the Tarot's way of saying now is not the time to focus on money, but rather on rest, quietness, and finding your balance. The ideas will flow again, once you have had a chance to still your mind and body. Like a car without fuel, there is only so much mileage you can cover before you run out of gas. Remember, the Tarot will try to communicate with you on an individual intuitive level too. You may look at the picture in the card and think *ah yes*, it confirms my thoughts about working with meditation, mindfulness, or even end-of-life care. Allow the cards to speak to you on a personal level; sometimes there will be a message which is very unique to you and your circumstances.

Other Books from Bennion Kearny

Success in the Year of the Pig

On the 5th of February 2019, the Chinese Year of the Pig snuffles, trots, and leaps into our lives. But this is no regular Year of the Pig, it is the Year of the Earth Pig (also known as the Brown Pig) and the last time that happened was in 1959.

When you understand what to expect from the coming year, you can develop your strategy to make the most of it. With your newfound knowledge, you can make the very best of the opportunities ahead.

What will the next 12 months bring to you? Does the Pig present your astrological animal with opportunities or challenges? So, whether your year animal gets on easily with the Pig, or has to work a little harder at the relationship, you can make 2019 a wonderful year to remember.

The Savvy Traveller Survival Guide

The Savvy Traveller Survival Guide offers practical advice on avoiding the scams and hoaxes that can ruin any trip.

From no-menu, rigged betting, and scenic taxi tour scams to rental damage, baksheesh, and credit card deceits – this book details scam hotspots, how the scams play out and what you can do to prevent them. *The Savvy Traveller Survival Guide* will help you develop an awareness and vigilance for high-risk people, activities, and environments.

Forewarned is forearmed!

The Hidden Whisper

Want to dive into the paranormal and learn about Extra Sensory Perception, Psychokinesis, Ghosts, Poltergeists and more, but don't know where to start?

The Hidden Whisper is the acclaimed paranormal thriller, written by real-life parapsychologist Dr. JJ Lumsden, which offers a rare opportunity to enter the intriguing world of parapsychology through the eyes of Luke Jackson. The poltergeist narrative is combined with extensive endnotes and references that cover Extra Sensory Perception, Psychokinesis, Haunts, Out of Body Experiences, and more.

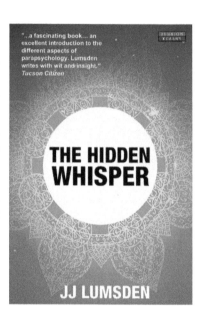

Finding Your Way Back to YOU: A self-help book for women who want to regain their Mojo and realise their dreams!

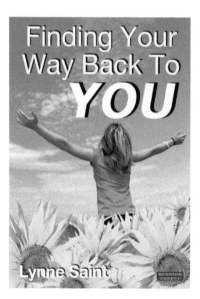

Are you at a crossroads in life, lacking in motivation, looking for a new direction or just plain 'stuck'?

Finding your Way back to YOU is a focused and concise resource written specifically for women who have found themselves in any of the positions above.

The good news is that you already have all of the resources you need to solve your own problems; this practical book helps you remove the barriers that prevent this from happening.

You Will Thrive: The Life-Affirming Way to Work and Become What You Really Desire

You Will Thrive addresses the subject of modern disillusionment. It is essential reading for people looking to make the most of their talents and be something more in life. Something that matters. Something that makes a difference in the world.

Through six empowering steps, it reveals 'the Way' to boldly follow your heart as it leads you to the perfect opportunities you seek. Through every step, it urges you to put a compelling thought to the test:

You possess the power within you to attract the right people, opportunities, and circumstances that you need to become what you desire.

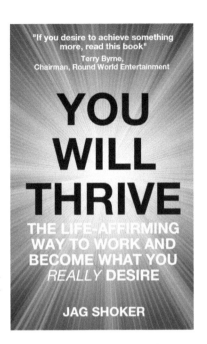

"If you desire to achieve something more, read this book"
Terry Byrne,
Chairman, Round World Entertainment

YOU WILL THRIVE

THE LIFE-AFFIRMING WAY TO WORK AND BECOME WHAT YOU *REALLY* DESIRE

JAG SHOKER

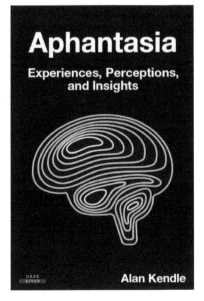

Aphantasia

Experiences, Perceptions, and Insights

Alan Kendle

Aphantasia: Experiences, Perceptions, and Insights

Close your eyes and picture a sunrise.

For the majority of people, the ability to visualize images – such as a sunrise – seems straightforward, and can be accomplished 'on demand'. But, for potentially some 2% of the population, conjuring up an image in one's mind's eye is not possible; attempts to visualize images just bring up darkness.

Put together by lead author Alan Kendle – who discovered his Aphantasia in 2016 – this title is a collection of insights from contributors across the world detailing their lives with the condition. It offers rich, diverse, and often amusing insights and experiences into Aphantasia's effects. For anyone who wishes to understand this most intriguing condition better, the book provides a wonderful and succinct starting point.

CPSIA information can be obtained
at www.ICGtesting.com
Printed in the USA
BVHW090808131120
593074BV00007B/334